How to Read
Your Mother's Mind

How to Read
Your Mother's Mind

James M. Deem

Illustrated by True Kelley

Houghton Mifflin Company
Boston 1994

For Susan
and her four mind-readers

— J.D.

Text copyright © 1994 by James M. Deem
Illustrations copyright © 1994 by True Kelley

Library of Congress Cataloging-in-Publication Data

Deem, James M.
  How to read your mother's mind / by James M. Deem ; illustrated by
True Kelley.
    p.   cm.
  Includes bibliographical references and index.
  Summary: Explores the myths and facts about extrasensory
perception, or ESP, relates the experiences of telepathic persons,
and explains how to develop your own ESP.
  ISBN 0-395-62426-6
  1. Extrasensory perception — Juvenile literature.   2. Psychic
ability — Juvenile literature. [1. Extrasensory perception.
2. Psychic ability.]   I. Kelley, True, ill.   II. Title.
BF1321.D44   1994   92-41351
133.8 — dc20   CIP
                        AC

Printed in the United States of America

VB   10 9 8 7 6 5 4 3 2 1

Contents

Glossary

clairvoyance — a type of ESP in which a person gathers information about an object, person, or event by receiving mental impressions.

parapsychologist — a person who studies events outside the range of normal experiences, such as ESP and apparitions.

parapsychology — a field of study involving paranormal events.

precognition — a type of ESP which involves the ability to foresee the future, usually through dreams.

psychic — a person who supposedly has a strong ESP ability. Often this person makes a living charging for psychic services.

telepathy — a type of ESP in which a person (the sender) somehow communicates outside normal communication channels with another person (the receiver). The communication is usually limited to a thought, feeling, or emotion, and often the sender is involved in a personal crisis.

Introduction

Have you ever known what your mother was going to say to you before she opened her mouth? Have you ever glanced at the telephone, knowing not only that it was about to ring but even the name of the caller? Have you ever woken up to find that you had the same dream as someone else in your family? Or, have you ever watched as a recent dream came true before your eyes?

If so, you've experienced the power of extrasensory perception, or ESP. According to many polls over the years, more than half of all Americans *believe* that ESP exists; some claim to have experienced it. But many people don't know exactly what ESP is. Does ESP help you predict the future or merely see the present? Does ESP allow you to discover the private thoughts in people's minds? Can ESP help you save your life or someone else's? Is there any proof that ESP is real, or does it have to be taken on faith alone?

How to Read Your Mother's Mind reviews the myths and the facts about ESP. Part I explains what ESP is, who has it, and how it works. Part II describes how you can develop your own ESPower. Throughout the book you will read true stories of people who have experienced ESP. You may choose to believe these stories or not, but all are supposed to have really happened. Whenever possible, I have given the names of the people who reported the experiences and the location of the events. Many people, however, decide against giving their names and addresses in order to protect their privacy. In some cases, I have provided names to make the stories easier to read. But I have not supplied dates or locations (when none were given). I have included dialogue only when it was contained in (or strongly suggested by) the original account.

If you have any ESPeriences after reading this book, please write me: James M. Deem, Houghton Mifflin Company, 222 Berkeley Street, Boston, Massachusetts, 02116.

Until then, have a happy and healthy future.

How to Read
Your Mother's Mind

Part I
The Essentials of ESP

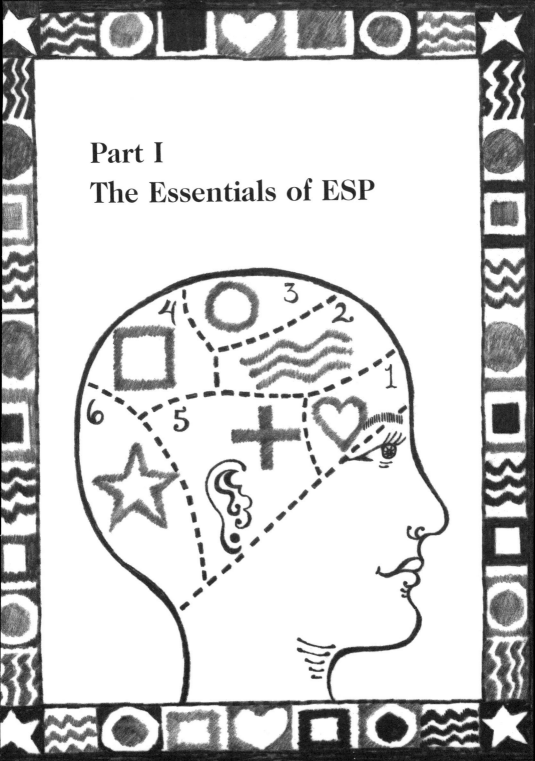

1. Misconceptions About ESPerception

What do you know about extrasensory perception, or ESP? Many people don't know exactly what the term means. As humans, we experience life through our five senses. We see, hear, taste, touch, and smell in order to gather knowledge about the world around us. But ESP appears to bypass these senses to provide us with information in an "extrasensory" (that is, beyond the five senses) way. Is ESP a "sixth sense" or a "second sight" (as it has been called)? Does it allow a person to see visions or to have dreams that foretell the future?

And who has ESP? Do you think of mind readers, spoon benders, or crystal-ball gazers? Do you visualize fortunetellers who advertise their services on signs and billboards ("Psychic Readings: Open 24 Hours") or

newspaper psychics whose predictions are announced in bold headlines. Do you conjure up images of telephone telepaths who charge $3.95 per minute to "read" the future?

Or, do you see someone quite like you?

Before you can think about reading your mother's mind (or anyone else's for that matter), you need to clear up any mistaken ideas you may have about ESPerception. Here are five common misconceptions:

ESP Misconception 1: ESP is usually a dramatic experience

Many people think that ESP gives advance warning about earthshaking, life-changing events. They have read about people who knew ahead of time that an airplane would crash ("I cancelled my reservation because I dreamed that something was going to happen to the plane") or that someone would be killed in an accident ("I dreamed that my cousin was going to die three days before it happened"). While this type of dramatic experience does happen occasionally, many ESP experiences (that is, ESPeriences) are usually so ordinary that people classify them as coincidences and forget about them.

For example, when he was four years old, Steve woke up screaming one night.

"What's wrong?" his mother asked, rushing into his bedroom.

"I dreamed about a snake," was all Steve said.

The next day, no one in the family talked about his dream, and Steve did not seem to be troubled. But that night — and the next — he awoke screaming. Both times, he told his mother that he had dreamed about a snake.

The next morning, after three nights of the same dream, Steve was playing in his backyard when he saw . . . a snake. But the snake wasn't dangerous, and Steve wasn't terrified. He simply watched until it slithered into some bushes. After that, he slept through the night, no longer bothered by the dream.

Steve's story, first described by parapsychologist Louisa Rhine of Duke University, captures both the mystery and the reality of ESP. Was Steve's three-night dream about the snake a coincidence? Or was his dream an

17

ESPerience: a glimpse at his future encounter with the snake?

His parents decided it was a coincidence. After all, it was unimportant. It wasn't as if he'd stumbled across a rattlesnake or a copperhead that bit him. He just saw a snake in his backyard. They believed — incorrectly — that a dream involving ESP had to be dramatic.

Two years later, though, they changed their minds when Steve began to have another series of dreams.

"What's the matter?" his mother asked when his screams woke her.

"I was falling into a hole."

"It was just a dream," she reassured him. "Don't worry. Go back to sleep."

But the dream returned — not for three nights, but for three weeks. Each night he saw himself falling into a bottomless hole; each night he woke screaming in terror.

On a snowy day, twenty-two days after his dream began, Steve was outside when his mother thought she heard him scream. Her heart jumped: Was he playing or was he in trouble? She opened the back door to listen.

This time the scream was clear. "Help!" he called. "Somebody help!"

His mother quickly found Steve in a neighbor's backyard. The top of an old septic tank had rotted through, and he had fallen into it. He was immersed in water up to his waist and sinking fast.

By the time he was rescued, he had sunk up to his shoulders and was moments away from drowning. That night, Steve did not dream about falling into a hole.

Was his three-week dream a coincidence? Or, was his dream advance information about his future misfortune with the septic tank? Did his second series of dreams help convince you, as it did his parents, that the snake dreams were ESPeriences, too?

Steve's dreams went from the ordinary to the dramatic. But notice that the "bottomless hole" dreams did not provide him with any information that might have prevented him from falling into the septic tank. In fact, ESP almost never allows a person to avoid or escape a future event. Steve's dreams show very clearly how real ESP works.

ESP Misconception 2: ESP only happens in dreams

Steve's dreams are not the only way that ESP has been observed in practice. It also occurs during our waking hours, as demonstrated in the following two cases:

Carmen's Feeling: Carmen, a nineteen-year-old, had recently moved to California to find a job. Quite by accident, she met Joe, a boy she had known in high school. When he asked her out, she accepted.

During their date, she suddenly felt an odd chill. Joe noticed a strange look on her face.

"What's wrong, Carmen?" Joe asked. "Are you sick?"

20

"You won't believe this," she said. "But I have the feeling that my grandmother just died."

Carmen had no reason to believe that something had happened. Her grandmother had been hospitalized after breaking her hip in a fall, but the doctors expected her to recover.

"Can you take me home?" she asked.

Joe dropped her off at her apartment building. As she walked in the front door, her landlady stopped her.

"Call this number," the landlady said. "There's a telegram for you."

Carmen dialed the number, and her mother's telegram was read to her: "Grandma is dead. Please come home."

Ed's Vision: A young Wisconsin boy named Ed was riding with his family one day.

"Did Aunt Myrtle and Uncle Charles have a wreck with a train?" he asked suddenly.

"What are you talking about?" his father asked.

"I see that they did," Ed told them.

The family went on with their drive and thought nothing more about his question. The next day, though, they received a telephone call from Myrtle and Charles.

"You won't believe what happened to us yesterday," Myrtle said. "We were coming home, and the car stalled on a railroad crossing."

Fortunately, they were able to escape from the car before an oncoming train rammed it. The accident had happened at the same time Ed had his vision.

Though there are other types of ESPeriences, the most common ones are similar to those reported by Steve, Carmen, and Ed. That is, they are dreams, feelings, or visions that either predict some future event or occur at the same time as an important event. When something happens that seems to be related to the dream or feeling or vision, many people choose to believe that their experiences were ESPeriences.

ESP Misconception 3: ESP isn't real

Some people think that ESP is a trick or a lie. They are certain that no such ability exists. These nonbelievers may not know, however, that there are three different sources of information which show the reality of ESP.

From the least to the most convincing, they are:

Information from surveys: In a recent study conducted on Americans and Western Europeans, the United States (followed closely by Italy and Iceland) headed the list of countries that report the most ESPeriences. According to researchers Erlendur Haraldsson and Joop Houtkooper, who conducted the survey, perhaps sixty percent of all Americans (around 145 million people) believe that they have had some type of ESPerience. Other surveys have reported similar findings. On the other hand, citizens of Denmark and Norway report many fewer ESPeriences.

Does ESP *really* happen more in certain countries? No one knows. All that can be said is that some cultures have stronger beliefs in ESP, and citizens of some countries report more ESPeriences.

Reports of ESPeriences: Surveys aren't the only source of information on ESP. Thousands of ESPeriences have been collected and published in books and magazine articles. Perhaps the most famous collector of ESP stories was Dr. Louisa Rhine. People wrote to Dr. Rhine describing unusual experiences, and she summarized their stories, grouped them into categories, and published them in her books.

The problem with ESP stories is that they don't provide proof that ESP is real for at least two reasons. First, many people report an ESPerience long after it has occurred. They rely on their *memory* of a distant ESPerience, which is a poor substitute for *immediate recall* of a recent ESPerience. Second, most people who report an ESPerience are never questioned about it to make sure that the details are clear and understandable. For example, an interviewer might have asked Steve for more details about his dreams and how well they matched the actual events. In Carmen's case, an interviewer might have encouraged her to describe more clearly the chill and feeling that let her know that her grandmother had just died. Moreover, an interviewer might have asked Ed to describe exactly what he saw in his vision. But even if someone reports a psychic experience immediately and is interviewed about its details, he or she cannot *prove* that the ESPerience was real. After all, someone could easily lie about having an ESPerience.

Of course, Dr. Rhine never set out to prove the existence of ESP; she merely wanted to collect the unusual experiences people *believed* they had had so that they could be used by researchers to conduct laboratory experiments about ESP.

Scientific evidence: Although ESP stories are often interesting, a scientist would have a difficult time believing an account that could not be observed or measured. For this reason, most parapsychologists have chosen to study ESP by experimenting in the laboratory, using conditions that eliminate the possibility of fraud and error. They have tested thousands of individuals for various types of ESP behavior and have published their findings in books and scientific journals.

24

According to Richard Broughton, director of research at the Institute of Parapsychology in Durham, North Carolina, scientific evidence does suggest that ESP has been consistently and significantly measured in the laboratory. But — and this is probably more important — the evidence also suggests that ESP is *not* a powerful ability in most people. In fact, ESP may be a lot like artistic and musical talent. Almost everyone seems to be born with some ability, but only a few people excel.

One type of experiment that has provided evidence that ESP is real is known as the *ganzfeld*. Every experiment begins with a *hypothesis*, or prediction, about the expected results. In ganzfeld experiments, scientists predicted that a person in a distraction-free room would be better able to pick up ESP signals.

Here's how a ganzfeld experiment is conducted: The person to be tested, called the subject, is asked to lie down in a soundproof room. Then the experimenter places half of a Ping-Pong ball over each of the subject's eyes. A red light is positioned overhead so that the subject can see only a pinkish haze filtering through the Ping-Pong ball halves. Headphones play soothing sounds (waves washing up on the seashore, for example), followed by instructions that help the subject relax. After fifteen minutes or so, the subject is ready for the experiment. The headphones begin to play something known as "white noise" (a neutral, distraction-free sound), and the subject is told to say whatever comes to mind.

In a nearby room, another person, called the sender, looks at a picture, trying to transmit it to the subject. In a ganzfeld experiment conducted in 1989 by parapsychologist Charles Honorton and anthropologist Marilyn Schlitz, Schlitz was elected to transmit a picture that she was watching on a computer screen. During the sixty seconds that it appeared on the screen, she was to concentrate on the image, trying to send it to Subject 332.

A GANZFELD EXPERIMENT

The subject lies down in a sound proof room.

red light

half Ping-Pong balls placed over eyes

Headphones play relaxation tape for about 15 minutes — then white noise.

The subject is told to say whatever comes to mind.

Meanwhile, in another room a sender tries to transmit a picture to the subject.

The sender

When Subject 332 was asked to describe what he visualized, he said:

There's a man with a dark beard and he's got a sharp face. . . .
There's another man with a beard. Now there's green and
white and he's in bushes. . . . He looks like Robin Hood and
he's wearing a hat. . . . I can see his hat and he has a sack
over his shoulder . . . and there's a billboard that says 'Coca-
Cola' on it. . . . There's a snowman again and it's got a carrot
for a nose and three black buttons coming down the front. . . .
There's a white beard again. There's a man with a white
beard . . . there's an old man with a beard.

What picture was Schlitz sending?

Taken from a 1950s magazine, it was an advertisement with an old-fashioned Santa Claus holding a bottle of Coke. The photograph shows the Santa from the waist up and includes three buttons on the front of his suit. Behind the Santa is a traditional Christmas tree hung with ornaments and a large bottle top with the words "Coca-Cola" leaning against the tree.

Compare Schlitz's picture with the images that Subject 332 saw, and the similarities are quite noticeable. He saw an old man with a white beard who was wearing a hat and carrying a sack, green bushes, the name of the soft drink, and three buttons. He also made some mistakes. At first, he saw a man in a dark beard; he also thought he saw a snowman with a carrot nose. Considering, however, that Schlitz could have been trying to send any picture, Subject 332's descriptions seem remarkably

28

on target. But the fuzziness of the images also indicates that ESP signals must be fairly weak, even when all other distractions are eliminated.

ESP Misconception 4: ESP is something new

ESP is not new at all: people have reported ESPeriences for more than two thousand years. For example, people who lived in the ancient civilizations of Mesopotamia and Egypt believed that dreams contained information about their health or their future. They hired experts to study and interpret their dreams, so that they could make decisions about how to lead their daily lives. Even

the Bible has many passages that describe experiences that seem to involve ESP.

But the scientific study of ESP *is* relatively new. In fact, no one applied science to ESP until about one hundred years ago. Even now, there have been few parapsychologists to carry out the work. Richard Broughton estimates that today there are only about fifty to be found in Europe, the United States, and all other English-speaking countries combined.

This lack of long-term scientific study has prevented the discovery of much information about how ESP works; scientific investigation takes time. Parapsychologists don't know whether the brain acts as a kind of radio transmitter and receiver, able to send and receive

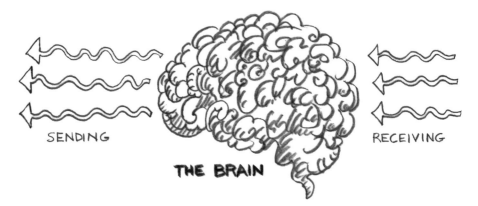

SENDING   RECEIVING

THE BRAIN

messages, or if some other process is at work. They also don't know why some individuals have many ESPeriences while others have none.

ESP Misconception 5: ESP is one process

Saying that ESP allows people to read minds or predict the future makes ESP sound quite simple. Actually, it is quite complicated. ESP is not one process; rather, it can involve three different types of perception: clairvoyance, telepathy, and precognition. The next two chapters explain how each works separately — and together.

2. Three ESPossibilities

Now that you know some important facts about ESP, it's time to fill in some of the details. If you ever have an ESPerience, you'll want to be able to determine which type of ESP was involved: clairvoyance, telepathy, or precognition.

ESPossibility 1: Clairvoyance

Clairvoyance (a French term meaning "clear seeing") occurs in two main ways. Sometimes it happens when a person gets *mental impressions* about a person, an object, a place, or an event. These impressions are usually in the form of dreams or waking visions that appear suddenly and without warning. Despite what the name implies, a clairvoyant impression will not be a clear, realistic mental picture; it will almost always be fuzzy and vague. Other times, clairvoyance occurs when the person just *knows* something about an object or event. Although clairvoyance makes no sense in a logical way, such experiences are regularly reported and have been tested successfully in parapsychology laboratories.

Clairvoyant visions. In the classic work *Phantasms of the Living,* Frederic Myers described a clairvoyant vision experienced by a ten-year-old English girl named Sarah. She was reading a math book as she walked down a country road when her surroundings suddenly disappeared and she could see her mother lying on the floor

of a spare room at home. The image was so vivid that she could even see a handkerchief with a lace border on the floor nearby. Sarah could not sense her mother's feelings or thoughts, but the vision suggested that her mother had become quite ill. Rather than run straight home, Sarah went to the local doctor and asked him to accompany her.

"Why should I?" he wanted to know.

"Because . . . because . . . my mother has been in good health. And she was supposed to have gone out today. Why would I see her so clearly lying on the floor if something wasn't so dreadfully wrong?"

When they arrived at her house, Sarah's father took one look at the doctor and asked, "Who's ill?"

"Mother," Sarah said. Then she led them to the upstairs room where her mother lay on the floor. She had had a heart attack, and the doctor told Sarah that she would have died if Sarah had not sought his help so promptly.

No one in the family realized that the mother had taken ill. And the lacy handkerchief, indeed, lay a few feet away from Sarah's mother.

Author Bernard Gittelson described a more unusual clairvoyant experience that involved neither a dream nor a vision, but sound and taste. Barbara was suddenly awakened one night by the sound of people screaming and the taste of smoke in her mouth. As soon as she sat up in bed, the noise and the taste disappeared. She

looked at the bedside clock, which read 3:40 A.M. Perhaps she had dreamed about the screaming and smoke, but she couldn't recall any dreams — only a short burst of yelling and a smoky taste. Still, she decided to take no chances and woke her husband. Together they checked the house to make sure nothing was on fire. When they found nothing wrong, they went back to bed.

The next night, as she watched the local news, she was surprised to hear that a factory had exploded some

90 miles away. The explosion killed six people and created a huge fire. Even more surprising was the fact that the explosion had occurred at exactly 3:40 A.M.

Clairvoyant knowledge. Louisa Rhine tells of an Oregon woman who took off her wedding and engagement rings to wash the dishes and placed them in a cupboard near the sink. She forgot about them until later that night, but when she went to retrieve them, they were gone. Although she and her husband looked everywhere, they could not locate the rings. In a letter to Dr. Rhine, the unnamed woman explained what happened next.

> Later that night, I was standing at the kitchen sink, trying to hold back my tears, when suddenly something told me to look in the ice-cube tray. I rushed to the refrigerator, pulled out the ice tray and there were my rings frozen in a cube of ice. I was so happy I rushed back to tell my husband. We started talking it over and he remembered coming into the house in the dark and without turning on the lights he opened the refrigerator, pulled out the ice tray for ice and reached for some glasses into the cupboard where my rings were. Then he filled the ice tray with water again and put it back in the refrigerator.

She went on to say that she had no good reason to suspect the ice tray. First, her husband had never replaced an ice tray before. Second, he hadn't known that her rings were on the shelf. He must have accidentally knocked them into the ice-cube tray without knowing what he had done. The woman concluded her letter: "I remember at the time I received the message or whatever it was, I had a funny sensation. What made me look in that ice tray?"

Psychometry. A special type of clairvoyance is called *psychometry.* Although the term literally means "soul measuring," it is often more accurately called "object-reading." A person using psychometry attempts to use clairvoyance to obtain information or knowledge about the history of an object.

A few clairvoyants prefer to hold the unfamiliar object in their hands, but most ask that it be wrapped in cloth and placed in a box to make sure that no one suspects them of trickery or fraud. They do not even hold the box, since clues might be obtained by the object's weight and its sound if the box is rattled.

The clairvoyant describes the impressions he or she reads from an object. The images are often vague and fleeting — rather than sharp photographs, they are fuzzy and even distorted. But if the clairvoyant is successful, these impressions give information about the object and the civilization or environment it came from.

USING PSYCHOMETRY

WHAT DOES HE "SEE" IN THE BOX?

ANSWER: AN APPLE

Count Giunasi, a member of the Italian nobility, appeared to have remarkable psychometric abilities. Around 1850, he met the poet Robert Browning, who was visiting Florence, at a dinner party. Browning, who was a well-known skeptic when it came to ESP, told the count that he doubted his "powers."

"Perhaps you have something with you — a memento of some sort — something you can hand me," he told Browning. "Then you can judge for yourself."

Browning did not usually wear jewelry or carry any mementos. That night, however, he was wearing a pair of gold cuff links that had come down to him from a great-uncle. He hesitated a moment, then handed one of the cuff links to the count. The count held it for a while, all the time studying Browning's face. Then he said, "There is something here that cries in my ear: Murder, murder!"

Browning was stunned: The cuff links had been worn by his great-uncle eighty years earlier on the night that he was murdered on St. Kitts, an island in the West Indies.

"What else can you tell me?" Browning asked.

"I see a bed in a room," was all he was able to add.

Despite the information that Giunasi gave — information he could not have known — Browning remained convinced that ESP was trickery. In a letter to the British Society for Psychical Research, Browning stated that he was certain Giunasi had somehow gathered clues from his face and eyes to assist him in his "reading." Even if Browning did convey some sense of doom when he handed the cuff links to Giunasi, what facial expression could have suggested the idea that the murder took place in a bedroom? Was Browning being too skeptical? Should he have accepted the encounter as real? And even if he didn't, should you accept it now as proof that ESP exists or ask for more evidence?

According to author Colin Wilson, Nelson Palmer is another user of psychometry. Surprisingly, Palmer didn't realize that he had such an ability until he was forty-nine years old. Even then, he hesitated to use his special skill since he was often asked to apply it in tragic situations. For example, in 1953 the Cohen family of Durban, South Africa, asked Palmer to help locate their six-year-old son, Leon, who had been kidnapped. What kind of object could help Palmer receive impressions about Leon? Although it may sound odd, he asked for the underwear that Leon had worn the day before the kidnapping.

Joined by a few police officers, Palmer went to work. Within a few moments, he began to describe an apartment building with a peculiar neon sign. A police officer

realized that the description fit a new building in Durban. Palmer then turned his attention to the appearance of the kidnappers; he sensed that there were two, a man and a woman. He described the man in vivid detail.

"That's John Kramer," one officer said automatically. John Kramer was well known for many other crimes.

The police followed Palmer's leads. They went to the building and discovered that Kramer and his wife had recently rented an apartment there. In it they found Leon Cohen, guarded by the Kramers, but uninjured.

ESPossibility 2: Telepathy

A second type of ESP, called telepathy, allows thoughts, feelings, or emotions to be transmitted quite unexpectedly from the mind of one person to another, usually during moments of crisis. Unlike clairvoyance, which gives information about physical things, telepathy provides information about someone's mental state.

Telepathy usually happens between two people who know each other, though they may not be close friends or even related. But it rarely gives complete information, merely a small piece. This fragment may not be enough to help a person make an exact connection to the person sending the message. Sometimes the information comes when the person is awake. Other times telepathy occurs while a person is dreaming.

Since one person is able to receive a mental message from another, people often mistakenly refer to it as "mind-reading." This suggests that telepathy is something a person can do at will; however, it simply doesn't work that way. Some scientists aren't even convinced that telepathy is a separate form of ESP; rather, they maintain telepathy is really clairvoyance; instead of seeing an object or place, the person is actually "seeing" the thoughts of another person.

Waking telepathy: physical sensation or emotion. Louisa Rhine described a telepathic experience that occurred between a young woman named Virginia and her father.

One Sunday night after dinner, her father went for a walk around their small farm. Virginia was concerned for him, especially since their home life was miserable at the time. Although it wasn't unusual for her father to take a walk, Virginia suddenly felt panicky: something was happening to him. She told Dr. Rhine in a letter describing the experience: "I have never felt such terror and extreme worry."

She didn't know where he had gone, but she tried to find him. She ran to all corners of their property and even checked with their neighbors. No one had seen him. When she realized that she would not find him, she decided to pray:

I went to a favorite tree and there alone I knelt and prayed for Father to be protected. I never prayed like that before. All at once my nerves quieted and I felt at ease as if something were lifted from me. I went back to the house. Quite a while later Dad came back.

He told Virginia that he had gone walking in some nearby woods and discovered an old abandoned barn. He began to explore the barn, when he heard a rattling sound. He turned and saw a large rattlesnake ready to strike. Quickly he grabbed a stone and an iron bar and killed the snake. Virginia's father's encounter coincided

with her own feeling of panic. Had she received a telepathic message from her father telling her that he was in danger?

Waking telepathy: a voice. Dr. Rhine also told the story of a young woman named Angela who had recently moved from her parents' house in New York to Los Angeles. On a Thursday night Angela heard her mother calling her from the next room.

"Angela," her mother said.

"Yes, Mother," Angela answered and waited for her mother to speak.

Then Angela realized her mistake and laughed at herself. Her mother wasn't with her; her mother was at home some 3,000 miles away. Angela decided that she must have imagined her mother's voice.

The next week she received a letter from her mother. Although Angela hadn't told her mother about her experience, her mother referred to that unusual Thursday night. "I was so lonesome for you," her mother wrote, "that I stood in the doorway of your bedroom and called to you."

Her mother had telepathically communicated with Angela.

Dream telepathy: incorporating an event. Dream telepathy often involves a dream that contains an actual event occurring at the same time as the dream. According to author B. Hoffman, a Soviet sailor named E. M. Kamintze became ill and the submarine he was assigned to had to leave port without him. Confined to the hospital, Kamintze had the following dream:

> I was right back on the submarine standing on the deck. The boat began to descend into the water, but I was unable to reach the conning tower and make my way down to the safety of the ship; I was overwhelmed by the water, began to swallow it, and felt that I was drowning. At this point I awoke sweating and with my pulse racing. I remembered the dream quite vividly afterward. When the submarine returned to the base and I rejoined the crew, I heard that one of my comrades had drowned. He had accidentally remained on deck while the boat submerged. When I checked the ship's log, I discovered that the accident had happened at the very moment I experienced the nightmare of my own drowning.

Dream telepathy: sharing a dream. Sometimes people can communicate telepathically in their dreams. Louisa Rhine described a Michigan woman whose son Clarence had recently left home to attend a university in another state.

One night the woman dreamed that she was sitting on one of the branches of a large pine tree. She heard someone walking through the woods and noticed a man who appeared to be lost. As he walked closer to her tree, she realized that he was her son. His clothes were torn, his face scratched and bleeding. She felt so sorry for him that she called down to him, "Clarence, go this way. Here is the path you must take." He looked up, saw her sitting in the tree, and smiled at her. Then he walked out of the forest, using the path she instructed him to take.

Later that same week, the woman received a letter from Clarence telling her about a strange and wonderful dream he had had. In the dream, he found himself lost, pushing his way through a dark, thick forest. He was worried that he would never reach the end of the forest.

Suddenly he heard a voice coming from above him that said, "Clarence, go this way." He followed the path the voice had indicated. The dream ended as he made his way out of the forest.

Shortly after this, he came home on vacation. His mother greeted him with the news that it was her voice he had heard. "I was up in the tree," she said.

Clarence was very surprised.

ESPossibility 3: Precognition

Precognition, which involves the extrasensory perception of an event before it happens, is the most common form of ESP. Precognition can involve either clairvoyance (seeing a future event or location) or telepathy (sensing someone's future feeling or thought).

People who have experiences that predict the future don't do so on a regular basis; they have an occasional dream or vision that later comes true. It's a very rare person (and, some would say, most likely a fraud) who has the repeated ability to predict the future accurately.

Most people who claim to predict the future regularly have a low success rate when all of their predictions are studied.

Sometimes a precognitive experience allows a person to hear a verbal warning regarding the future. A woman walking down the street may hear a voice shouting her name and stop. If she can't see the person who called her name and if a concrete block then crashes to the sidewalk in front of her — a place she might have been had she not stopped — the voice provided a precognitive warning. But the most frequent precognitive warning is a vision or dream that allows a person to see a small part of a future tragedy or other crisis.

Whether it's a voice, a vision, or a dream, a precognitive experience is often confusing or hard to understand until the event occurs. And perhaps the most troubling aspect of precognition is this: if someone "sees" that an accident will occur, why can't that person prevent it from happening? Since precognitive information is usually sketchy at best, it may not even make sense until this glimpse of the future becomes a reality.

Precognitive warnings: voices. In her autobiography, Winston Churchill's wife recounted a number of precognitive experiences that her famous husband believed he had had. As prime minister of Great Britain during World War II, Churchill had the habit of going out to greet the civil defense forces during air raids. It was customary for his chauffeur to open the rear passenger door on the driver's side so Churchill could enter the car. But one night, as the driver held the door open, Churchill walked around the car and, without explaining his action, climbed in on the opposite side. That night as they sped through darkened London, German bombs dropping everywhere, one exploded near the car, lifting the driver's side off the road. Instead of rolling over, and probably killing the driver and Churchill both, the car righted itself; they continued on their way.

"That was a near one," Churchill, a portly gentleman, joked. "It must have been my beef on this [side] that brought the car back down."

When his wife heard about the incident, she asked why he had decided to sit on the other side of the car that night.

"I don't know, I don't know," he told her.

His wife stared at him, waiting for an answer.

"Yes, I do know," he admitted finally. "When I got to the . . . door held open for me, something in me said, 'Stop, go round to the other side and get in there,' and that is what I did."

Although Churchill may not have had a vision of the exploding bomb and the rolling car consciously, he believed that he had received information that saved his life.

Precognitive warnings: visions. According to parapsychologist Louisa Rhine, Evelyn had a vision of her oldest son, Herbert, lying dead in the bathtub. Although she didn't tell Herbert about her vision, she told her younger son Peter about it. In some ways, it seemed like a silly vision to her, since Herbert was a teenager and hardly in need of her care. But it had been so vivid she couldn't forget it. A few years later, Herbert moved out of the house, but came back occasionally. During one visit, she heard him singing and whistling as he took a bath. She had an appointment and was ready to leave the house, but the memory of the bathtub vision stopped her. Perhaps she was being foolish, but she couldn't leave as long as he was in the tub. Shortly, she heard the water draining from the tub. And she waited. When she failed to hear any further noises, she knocked on the door.

"Is everything all right?" she asked.

When Herbert didn't answer, she opened the door and found him unconscious in the empty bathtub, exactly the way she had envisioned it. The gas heater in the bathroom had apparently malfunctioned, filling the room with deadly fumes. She turned off the heater, opened the windows, and called the doctor. By paying attention to her vision, she managed to save her son's life.

Precognitive warnings: dreams. At one point in his life, author Samuel Langhorne Clemens (otherwise known as Mark Twain) worked with his brother Henry on the *Pennsylvania*, a riverboat that ran between New Orleans and St. Louis. One night, when the two young men were visiting their sister Pamela in St. Louis, Clemens had a disturbing dream. He dreamed that Henry had died, and as was common at the time, his body was lying in state in his sister's sitting room. The images in the dream were quite memorable. First, Clemens noticed that Henry's body had been placed in a metal casket that was supported by two chairs. Second, he observed some flowers on Henry's chest; all were white except for a single red flower in the center of the bouquet.

When Clemens awoke, he was so confused by the dream that he thought his brother had actually died. He dressed, preparing to observe his brother's body in the sitting room, but decided to take a walk. It was only during his walk that he realized he had been dreaming.

A few weeks later, Clemens and his brother were in New Orleans waiting for the *Pennsylvania* to return upriver. Because of a disagreement with the ship's pilot, Clemens decided to follow two days later on another boat. This would be the first time that the brothers had worked separate boats. The night before the *Pennsylvania* sailed, Clemens may have remembered his dream, for he found himself giving Henry some advice:

> In case of accident, whatever you do, don't lose your head — the passengers will do that. Rush for the hurricane deck and to the lifeboat, and obey the mate's orders. When the boat is launched, help the women and children into it. Don't get in yourself. The river is only a mile wide. You can swim ashore easily enough.

Unfortunately, the advice was useless.

On the return trip, Clemens's boat docked at Greenville, Mississippi, where he heard the tragic news: "The *Pennsylvania* is blown up just below Memphis, at Ship Island. One hundred and fifty lives lost!"

Four of the eight boilers on the *Pennsylvania* had exploded. Many people had been killed immediately; others had been scalded and suffered painful, lingering deaths. At first, the newspapers reported that Henry had escaped injury; later, Clemens discovered that his brother had been scalded. By the time he reached Memphis, Clemens learned that Henry had died.

Most of the dead were placed in unpainted wooden coffins, but not Henry. Because he was so young and handsome, and perhaps because he had suffered so much before he died, a special collection was taken to provide him with a metal coffin. When Clemens saw his brother's body in the casket, he was reminded of his dream. The scene was exactly as he had dreamed it, except for the fact that there were no flowers. Then, as he watched, a woman entered the room and placed a bouquet of white flowers on Henry's chest. A single red rose was at its center.

Was Twain's dream precognitive? Ian Stevenson, a psychiatrist at the University of Virginia, believes that it was, for two reasons. First, as is often the case, the dream concerned the death of a close relative. Second, it contained details that no one could have predicted (the metal coffin, the red rose). Of course, there were discrepancies, too, which is also common in precognitive dreams. Clemens dreamed of his brother's body in St. Louis, not Memphis. But the change in location does not detract from the remarkable details in Clemens's dream.

3. Determining Your GESP-IQ

GENERAL EXTRA SENSORY PERCEPTION

DO **YOU** HAVE IT ?

True ESP stories rarely involve one specific type of ESP; instead, they often overlap. For this reason, some parapsychologists prefer to use the term GESP, or general extrasensory perception, to describe complex ESP cases.

Read the following case reported by author Bernard Gittelson, and then try to determine which type of ESP is involved:

A pilot was practicing some difficult maneuvers in her Piper Cub one day in 1956. Suddenly she felt that something was wrong — not with the airplane but on the ground. She doubted this strange feeling, though, and pushed it from her mind and continued to practice. But the feeling kept returning, each time breaking her concentration.

Finally, she stopped practice and gave in to the feeling. She flew seventy miles off her intended course and noticed a car that had gone off a deserted country road. Without hesitating, she landed the small plane on the road and ran to the car. There, she pulled an unconscious woman from behind the wheel.

As she dragged the woman away from the car, the gas tank exploded and the car burst into flames. She laid the woman on the ground, only then realizing that the woman was her mother.

ESP appears to have been involved in this remarkable episode — but what kind? How did the pilot know that there was trouble on the ground? And how did she locate her mother's car?

If you chose telepathy, you may be correct. Since telepathy involves the communication of thoughts between two people who know each other, the mother may have been able to communicate telepathically with her daughter. However, the daughter had no idea that the message was sent by her mother.

If you chose clairvoyance, you may also be correct. The pilot had an *impression* of the landscape she should find.

If you chose precognition, you may also be correct. It's possible that the pilot's feeling that *something was wrong* might have been a feeling that *something worse might happen* (the explosion of the gas tank). Rather than having ESP about the car accident, she may have had ESP about the impending explosion.

It's also possible that telepathy, clairvoyance, and precognition were each involved. So it may be safest to say that this experience involved GESP.

Here's another story to analyze. This one, from Frederic Myers's book *Human Personality*, describes a strange experience that Dr. D. J. Parsons had in Sweet Springs, Missouri. On the way to dinner one night in 1889 with his nephew John, Dr. Parsons was stopped by a man who needed some medical help. Dr. Parsons told the man to come to his office in the morning. Later, troubled by the man's condition, Parsons decided to stop by his office to consult a medical book about the case. According to Dr. Parsons, who wrote to Myers, this is what happened as he and his nephew approached the office:

> Just as I stepped upon the door sill of the drug store in which my office is situated, some invisible influence stopped me instantly. I was much surprised, felt like I was almost dazed, the influence was so strong, almost like a blow. I felt I could not make another step. I said to my nephew, 'John, I do not like going into the office now, you go and read Flint and Atkins on the subject.' He went, lighted the lamp, took off his hat, and just as he was reaching for the book the report of a large pistol was heard [outside]. The ball entered the window near where he was standing, passed near to and over his head, struck the wall and fell to the floor. Had I been standing where he was, I would have been killed, as I am much taller than he.

Compare this story to the pilot's story and you can see some similarities. First, both were overcome by a strong feeling that guided them (toward a car accident or away from the office). Both witnessed a potentially harmful experience (the explosion and the pistol shot). But which types of ESP were involved?

Telepathy? Perhaps, if the person who shot the pistol, someone that Parsons knew, communicated his intentions telepathically before he shot the bullet.

Clairvoyance? Perhaps, especially if Dr. Parsons somehow had a vision of the person ready to shoot the gun.

Precognition? Yes, if he saw the bullet shattering the window or hitting the wall.

Or could it have involved a combination of the three? Perhaps the doctor's nephew had a precognitive vision that someone was about to shoot a gun in their direction and communicated that message to his uncle telepathically.

Confused? It's also possible that Dr. Parsons experienced heartburn after dinner, and it was sheer coincidence that he did not step into the office that night. Without more information the truth can never be known. So rather than try to pinpoint the precise type of ESP, it's wiser to say that Dr. Parsons's story suggests the presence of GESP.

As you can see, understanding the three basic types of ESP and analyzing an ESP encounter can be tricky. Now that you know what's involved, you're ready to test your GESP-IQ.

Imagine that two children are in a room, ready to begin an ESP experiment similar to one described by Charles Tart in his book *PSI*. Chloe has been told to think of an easy object to draw. After she draws it, she is to concentrate for thirty seconds on sending the image to David's mind. At the end of that time, David is to draw any image that appeared in his mind.

CHLOE'S PICTURE

DAVID'S PICTURE

Now read these statements about the experiment:

The General ESP-IQ Test

Choose one of the following for each statement:
- a. true
- b. false
- c. uncertain

1. ESP was responsible for the results of the experiment.
2. Chloe used telepathy to send the picture to David.
3. David used clairvoyance to receive an impression of the drawing.
4. David used telepathy to receive Chloe's thoughts about the drawing.
5. David used precognition to see the drawing that Chloe was going to make.
6. Something other than ESP caused the two drawings to be similar.
7. Coincidence was responsible for the results of the experiment.
8. The two drawings are not really similar.
9. David cheated and peeked at Chloe's drawing.
10. The results of the experiment prove that ESP is not possible.

Turn the page to find the answers and, most important, their explanation:

Question 1: ESP ?

It's **uncertain** that ESP was responsible for the results of the experiment. Something else may have caused the results.

Question 2: TELEPATHY ?

It's **uncertain** that Chloe used telepathy to send the picture to David. She may have used telepathy, but simply thinking about a picture does not mean that telepathy is taking place.

Questions 3–5: CLAIRVOYANCE TELEPATHY PRECOGNITION ?

It's **uncertain** that David used clairvoyance, telepathy, or precognition to get information about Chloe's drawing since they may not have followed the experiment exactly. If his experience was clairvoyant, he had an impression of travel involving a wheeled object. If it was telepathic, he received a message from Chloe's mind as she drew the car. If it was precognitive, David made his drawing before Chloe even decided what she was going to draw. It is also possible that none of the above occurred and their drawings were still similar.

Question 6:  **SOMETHING ELSE?**

It's **uncertain** that something else caused the two drawings to be similar, but the possibility cannot be ruled out. Suppose that the room used in the experiment had an open window facing a street. Moments before the experiment began, a vehicle with a noisy engine drove by. It is possible that both Chloe and David reacted to the noise subconsciously — and somewhat differently. The engine noise may have reminded Chloe of a sports car, while David associated it with a motorcycle.

Question 7: **COINCIDENCE?**

It is **uncertain** that coincidence caused the results of the experiment. As Charles Tart points out, people from the same culture often think alike. If David and Chloe are from a community that uses many cars and motorcycles, their drawings might simply be a coincidence. If they lived in a rural area of a developing country where there were no mechanized forms of transportation, their drawings might be more difficult to explain as coincidence.

Question 8: SIMILAR ?

It is **uncertain** that the two drawings are not similar, since this is a matter of individual judgment. Because both sketches portray vehicles, they have some points in common. Both have similar wheels and headlights. On the other hand, there are many differences between the two vehicles. A stickler for details would say that David's motorcycle doesn't really resemble Chloe's sports car except in two minor ways.

Question 9: CHEATED ?

It is **uncertain** that David cheated and peeked at Chloe's drawing. Since we don't know how or where they were sitting in the room, this possibility must be considered.

Question 10: IMPOSSIBLE ?

False. The results of the experiment prove nothing. ESP may or may not be possible, but this experiment allows three types of ESP to be confused and doesn't rule out other possibilities.

As you go through the rest of this book, be on the lookout for the types of ESP involved in each of the stories. Then ask yourself questions about them to sharpen your thinking skills.

4. Psychics

People with excellent ESP ability often call themselves "psychics." Usually they prefer to lead normal lives, choosing not to let most people know that they have ESPower. Even if someone asks for their help, they rarely charge for their services and offer assistance only when they feel it will be helpful. They don't attempt to predict the future or offer advice based on what they "see."

Some others choose to be professional psychics — they open their own ESP business and charge money to help people with questions or personal problems. Some use only ESPower; others advertise a variety of methods to foretell the future, such as palmistry, astrology, and tea-leaf readings. A few become famous enough that they are paid to provide regular predictions to tabloid newspapers.

There are at least three problems with professional psychics. First, their emphasis on "seeing into the future" turns ESP into just a source of predictions. This encourages many people to think of ESP as a strange power that can guide them through their lives. As you know by now, this is not the case. A second problem with professional psychics is that no psychic is correct all of the time. But professional psychics can't afford to be wrong very often; otherwise, they'd go out of business. Therefore, it is important to approach their predictions with healthy suspicion: are they really using their ESPower or are they simply using their powers of reasoning? For example, any professional psychic who claims that there will be an earthquake in California sometime during the next six months may be taking a good guess rather than seeing the future.

This leads to the third problem: many professional psychics are definitely fakes, with no ESPower. They merely use the name to trick people and make money.

If you wonder how you might tell the difference between a pseudo-psychic and a real one, authors Arthur Lyons and Marcello Truzzi suggest that you pay attention to the following "tricks":

Does the psychic use general statements that could fit many people? A pseudo-psychic may begin by saying something like this:

You have many questions. That's why you have come here today. But you have something important on your mind, something you want to Know, something that causes you great concern.

Sound good? Perhaps, but almost anyone going to a psychic has questions of great concern and perhaps one or two specific problems that outshadow all others. It doesn't take psychic talent to know this.

Does the psychic fish for information? A pseudo-psychic may try to get you to volunteer information. He or she may say, "I see a woman in your life" and pause. Most people have "a woman" in their lives. A pseudo-psychic hopes that you'll provide information and forget that you've provided it.

I see a woman in your life ...

Mom!

Does the psychic merely rely on her or his powers of observation and reasoning? A pseudo-psychic can pick up a great deal of information just by looking at your appearance (your clothes and hair style) and your demeanor (the way you hold your body and your mannerisms). Your hands alone can provide many clues. Are your fingers dirty or clean? Are your fingernails bitten down to

the quick or cut to a moderate length? Are your palms sweaty? Are your hands soft or calloused? By quickly looking you over and deciding what type of person you are, a pseudo-psychic can present you with information that may sound amazing but is, in fact, based strictly on good observation skills.

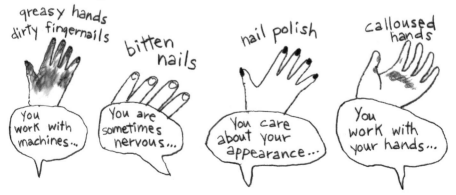

Does the psychic give too little or too much information? A pseudo-psychic can say, "I see you sitting in a car," hoping that you will add, "Oh, yes, last week we drove to my aunt Marcia's house." Instead, consider asking

the psychic, "What color is the car? Who else is in the car? Where is it going? Why is this important?"

On the other hand, a pseudo-psychic can overwhelm you with a large amount of information presented quite quickly. Rather than concentrate on it all, your mind focuses on the few bits that seem accurate. The rest may be totally false, but you go away believing that the psychic has given you valuable information.

Does the psychic predict things that are bound to come true anyway? "I see travel in the near future" or "You will come into some money soon" are two statements that can come true without much trouble. Notice that both statements are quite vague (travel where? when? with whom? how much money? when will I come into it? how will this happen?). As a result, they can easily come true.

I see you reading a book in the near future... its about ESP! Something about mothers. You look at a picture on page 70!

Of course, real psychics can also give vague impressions. In the rest of this chapter you'll read about five psychics. Judge for yourself whether their talents are real or not.

Psychic 1: Black Elk

Shamans, or medicine men and women, are a good example of a type of psychic many people never consider. According to D. Scott Rogo, a shaman has powers to diagnose and heal illness, control the weather, and use clairvoyance.

BLACK ELK

The last great medicine man of the Oglala Sioux was Black Elk. He was born on the Little Powder River in December 1862. When he was old and almost blind, his story was recorded by author John Neihardt in the book *Black Elk Speaks*. It includes an unforgettable episode that involved Black Elk and the weather.

After telling Neihardt about his first vision, Black Elk and a group of friends took him to the hilltop in South Dakota where it had occurred many years before.

"Something should happen today," Black Elk told Neihardt. "If I have any power left, the thunder beings of the west should hear me when I send a voice, and there should be at least a little thunder and a little rain."

Neihardt didn't see how that was possible: the day was sunny and the area was suffering from a severe drought. Black Elk wasn't bothered. He prepared himself by dressing in ceremonial clothes and painting his face. Then he began to speak to the spirits. Up until

the moment that Black Elk finished speaking, the sky was clear. Then it changed.

"We who listened now noted that thin clouds had gathered about us," Neihardt wrote later. "A scant chill rain began to fall and there was a low, muttering thunder without lightning."

Psychic 2: Eileen Garrett

Considered by many to be one of the greatest psychics of the twentieth century, Eileen Garrett was at one time the president of the Parapsychology Foundation and active in the field.

When she was four years old, she discovered her psychic ability. That's when she met The Children for the first time. The Children were two girls and a boy who visited her daily until she was about thirteen. She communicated with them without words, sometimes for

hours, sometimes only briefly. In her autobiography, Garrett described an aunt's reaction:

> When I told my aunt about The Children in the early days of their coming, she ridiculed the idea of my playmates whom she had neither heard nor seen. . . . "But come and see them for yourself," I begged. "That will do now," she told me coldly. "I've no time to waste on your fancies. Just try to touch one of these children. You'll find there's nothing to touch."
>
> The Children laughed when I told them that my aunt did not believe that they existed. "We are wiser than she is," they confided. It was easy for me to believe this, for I knew that they did indeed exist and that Aunt was mistaken.

Whenever she tried to explain The Children, "no one ever understood," she wrote.

Garrett was unlike many psychics in that she had different types of ESPower: telepathy, clairvoyance, and something known as "trance mediumship," a psychic state in which she believed that her visions were guided by spirits of the dead. Whether or not that is possible, many have no doubt that Garrett was gifted with ESP.

For example, during World War I she met and married a young soldier. When it was time for him to return to the war, he had a feeling that he would be killed. His premonition was correct.

The night that he died, Mrs. Garrett was having dinner with some friends when she had a vision of her husband being killed in an explosion. She reported the experience this way:

I became ill and begged to be excused. A few days later, I was advised by the War Office that he was among the missing. His brother officers later wrote that he had gone on a wire-cutting expedition and never returned.

No one ever knew exactly what had happened to him — except Garrett through her clairvoyant vision.

Psychic 3: Stefan Ossowiecki

Stefan Ossowiecki (pronounced Osso-viet-ski) was born in Moscow in 1877 and displayed no unusual abilities — at first. He worked as a chemical engineer. It wasn't until he was in his forties and living in Warsaw, Poland, that he became known as a great psychometrist.

He developed such a reputation that many noted scientists, including Nobel Prize–winning physiologist Charles Richet, became his friends and supporters. He also participated in many experiments that were conducted by noted parapsychologists of the day.

In 1935 he participated in an unusual psychometry experiment created by a Hungarian named Mr. Jonky. Jonky placed an object in a box, sealed it carefully, and gave it to a group of scientists. He told the scientists that after he had been dead for eight years, they were to invite a clairvoyant to "read" the object in the box. Jonky wanted to create the perfect test of psychometry to prove that it was a real skill, since after such a long time telepathy should be impossible. After all, Jonky had reasoned, how could a psychic receive information from the mind of a man who had been dead for eight years?

Eight years after Jonky's death, Ossowiecki was invited to "read" the box. In front of fifty scientists, he looked at the box and described what he sensed: "There is something here that pulls me to other worlds . . . to another planet." He believed that the box contained a small meteorite — along with some sugar.

When the box was opened, the scientists found that it did indeed contain a meteorite. Jonky had wrapped it in a piece of paper from a box of candy. Pieces of confectioners' sugar were still stuck to the paper. According to those present, Ossowiecki had performed an incredible feat.

Another astounding accomplishment, described by author Jeffrey Goodman, took place when Ossowiecki was approached by a man who wanted to locate the body of his brother, a Polish soldier. He had been killed in battle and buried along with seven hundred men in a mass grave. The family wanted to remove the body from the grave site and return it to a cemetery near the family's home. Not only did Ossowiecki draw a map indicating precisely where the soldier was buried, he described his fatal wounds.

Of course, you may wonder if Ossowiecki could possibly have been right. That's what the soldier's family wanted to know as well. So they asked Ossowiecki to assist them in exhuming the body. According to Goodman, Ossowiecki walked

> back and forth along the borders of the mass grave site. Suddenly he stopped, pointed down and declared that the body lay before him. The spot tallied with the one he had pinpointed earlier on his drawing. The digging began and at first it seemed that Ossowiecki might have been in error as body after body was removed from the site. Then he spoke again. The next body to be disinterred would be the dead brother, he declared. It was! Although the body, like the others, was badly mangled, identification was possible because the build, army rank, clothing and a gold crown on one of the teeth all matched the description of the dead man.

During World War II when Poland was occupied by German troops, Ossowiecki used his psychic ability, too. According to author Brian Inglis, Ossowiecki was able to warn others of danger. However, his saddest psychic accomplishment was the prediction he made one day in July 1944.

"I will soon be killed," he told his wife. "But I have had a wonderful life."

As the war drew to a close and Soviet and Allied troops began to liberate Poland, many Poles rebelled against the German army. In August 1944, Ossowiecki was taken prisoner along with some ten thousand other Polish men; all were executed. Author Stephan Schwartz described his death this way:

A squad of soldiers marched out; machine guns were set up. There were almost ten thousand people. The massacre took all that day and part of the next. Gun barrels melted and had to be replaced. When it was over, the bodies were soaked in gasoline and set ablaze.

But Ossowiecki's work lived on, recorded in manuscripts that his wife managed to save. Of course, no actual proof of his feats exists, and as a result, many scientists have difficulty believing all of his self-reported psychic adventures.

Psychic 4: Peter Hurkos

Celebrated psychic Peter Hurkos led two lives. The first was as Pieter van der Hurk, an ordinary Dutch citizen. On July 10, 1941, when he was thirty-one years old, he slipped from a ladder while painting and was knocked unconscious for four days. When he awoke, he found out that he had a broken shoulder, a brain concussion, and psychic ability that would change his life forever.

One day he told his wife, who was visiting him in the hospital, "Go and get Benny! The whole room is burning!" She ran home, but their son Benny was fine.

Five days later, however, their house caught on fire, and firefighters saved Benny from the flames. That precognitive experience began a long career in both psychic criminology and show business, which included a name change to Peter Hurkos.

Not everyone accepted Hurkos's ESPower. Authors Arthur Lyons and Marcello Truzzi report one of Hurkos's most embarrassing cases in their book *The Blue Sense*. In 1975 he was invited to appear on the television show *The Ashman File*. Chuck Ashman, who hosted the show, handed Hurkos a shirt that he said had belonged to Jimmy Hoffa, a leader of the Teamsters union who was supposedly killed by the Mafia; his body has never been found. Hurkos held the shirt and began to describe the last few days of Hoffa's life as well as the location of his body.

When the show ended, Ashman turned to the audience and said that the shirt was his, not Hoffa's. He asked viewers: How could Hurkos have received psychic impressions from something that was in no way related to Hoffa?

Psychic 5: Irene Hughes

Like Eileen Garrett, Irene Hughes says that her psychic ability occurs when "spirits" talk to her. She grew up in a Tennessee log cabin, aware that her mother had special psychic powers; she read coffee grounds to get her psychic impressions.

78

When Hughes was four, she talked to what she thought was a fairy; later she realized that it must have been a spirit. The spirit told her when people were going to visit or when family members would return home or when she would receive a letter. She describes her clairvoyance in this way:

I see a very clear mental image sometimes, just like watching a movie, except it seems to me that I'm very close and an observer. Sometimes I feel I'm a participant in the action, even though it may not have anything to do with me, like an international situation. Then I do use psychometry when I'm working on police cases and I make predictions of what will happen based on that.

I know that I pick up thoughts by telepathy occasionally, but I can tell the difference, so that I don't make a prediction based on a thought unless I see clairvoyantly that it is going to happen.

Since Hughes was fifteen, she has kept prediction notebooks, where she recorded the impressions she received. Eventually, she wrote a psychic newspaper column. Although Hughes often publishes her predictions, their success or failure is not always clear.

Some of her predictions have been too vague to judge.

For example, in a 1972 interview she predicted that, by 1982,

> a new monetary system for the United States will come into being . . . Many nations will enter into a cooperative structure that will lead to a world monetary system. How easy it will then be to travel — no cash, no checks, just a card to symbolize money.

Although someone may say that this prediction did not come to pass, another could choose to believe that Mrs. Hughes was referring to the spread of the credit card industry. Was Hughes using her psychic powers or her knowledge of business affairs?

Some predictions were unsubstantiated by others. She said that she predicted the assassination of Robert Kennedy. One day a newspaper reporter asked her quite unexpectedly, "What's going to happen to Bobby Kennedy?"

"He's going to be shot," Hughes answered.

Notice that Hughes's clairvoyant impression is very vague (where was Robert Kennedy when he was shot? who shot him? when did it occur?). Notice, too, that the encounter is not dated and the reporter is unnamed. Without this specific information, her experience cannot be verified.

Some of her predictions never happened. Authors Lyons and Truzzi noted one that was clearly off the mark. In 1981, she once wrote, the United States would put a satellite in orbit that would "generate enough energy to solve the world's oil crisis." Nothing of the kind occurred.

Finally, some of her predictions are still waiting to come true. By the year 2026, she once wrote, the United States Constitution will no longer exist, replaced by a new document and a new type of government. Could Hughes be right? Perhaps. She concluded this prediction by saying that

> in 2026, man will be much happier than he is today, and he will have more freedom in all areas of life. Man will live in greater trust and in greater love of his fellow man at that time than at any other era of history.

These are thoughts that almost anyone would like to believe. Whether they constitute psychic power or wishful thinking is another story altogether.

5. Using ESP

Can it be harnessed?

By now, you might be wondering if ESP can be harnessed and put to use in our daily lives. The answer is yes — and no. ESP has been applied in creative and unusual ways. Although some of the results have been disappointing, others seem to be downright extraordinary.

THE CASE OF THE COOKIE THIEF

COOKIES

ESP Use 1: Psychic criminology

Perhaps the most popular use of ESP is psychic criminology. That is, some psychics try to help police solve crimes by providing information about the crime, the perpetrator, or the victim. Sometimes this information leads to an arrest, but more often it docs not.

Private investigators Whitney Hibbard and Raymond Worring say that most law enforcement agencies have probably had at least one experience with a psychic, but won't admit it for fear that they will be ridiculed. For this reason alone, police departments don't seek out psychic help; usually psychics volunteer their services or members of a victim's family contact a psychic for help.

Police departments are not eager to become involved in psychic investigations for a number of other reasons. First, psychics provide unusual (and sometimes unhelpful) information, which can confound police investigators. For example, Hibbard and Worring describe the case of a missing boy who was thought to have drowned in a nearby river. Despite an intensive search, the police had not been able to find his body. Consequently, they turned to two psychics for assistance.

"All I can see is a snake, a motorcycle in the brush, and a man in a canoe," the first one told the police. An interesting vision, but it was of little use in pinpointing the location of the boy's body.

The second psychic said, "Go up the river exactly six miles from town and you'll find the body." These directions led an officer right to the body. Interestingly enough, as the officer approached the river, a snake slithered across the path in front of him. As he continued down the path, he saw a motorcycle hidden in the bushes. And when he found the body at the edge of the river, he glanced up and saw a man canoeing by.

Unlike the second psychic's vision, the first psychic's vision was not clairvoyant; rather she had had a precognitive vision of the officer locating the body. Although such an experience is interesting, it was of no value in helping the police find the boy.

Perhaps the main reason police avoid psychics is that even if a psychic can identify the perpetrator of a crime, evidence that proves this must also be uncovered. Psychics cannot go into court and testify that they "know" who killed someone or who robbed a bank. Their testimony would be judged hearsay and therefore inadmissible as evidence.

For example, psychic Nancy Anderson was asked by investigators to help identify a murder suspect. After she looked at photographs of the corpse, she told the police officers how the crime was committed, where the body had been found, and who the murderer was. The problem was that the police already had this information and even had the suspect she identified in custody. They were looking for proof that the suspect was connected to the murder, but Anderson's psychic impressions provided none. And her comments raised an interesting question: Was she having clairvoyant impressions or was she instead tuning in to the minds of the investigators who were in the room at the time of her reading?

Although psychic criminology usually involves persons working outside the police department, some police officers have been known to use their own well-developed ESP abilities in their investigations. According to Hibbard and Worring, some years ago one patrol officer had an extraordinary ability to detect illegal drugs in passing cars. While he was using radar to check for speeding cars, his own "psychic radar" determined which cars also contained drugs. He would stop the cars spotted both by radar and his ESP and search them for drugs. Although such searches are illegal today, at that time the officer had a high rate of arrest for illegal drug possession, supposedly because of his ESPower.

Another example of an officer with psychic ability was described by author Tom Dempsey. One day, responding to a burglary-in-progress call with his partner, Officer Bill Gros sensed that they were in danger. When Gros entered a rear bedroom, though nothing had been disturbed, the feeling became stronger. As in the other rooms of the house, the closet door was closed; everything was silent. But Gros was certain that the suspect was armed and hiding there.

He silently pointed to the door. His partner nodded. They positioned themselves on either side of the closet.

Then Gros said loudly, "We know you're in there. Come on out with your hands up."

Without warning, the suspect burst from the closet, holding a butcher knife. Alerted to the dangerous situation by his "sixth sense," Gros and his partner were able to disarm the suspect and take him into custody.

ESP Use 2: Psychic archaeology

Another way that ESP has been put to use is through psychic archaeology. Archaeological digs can be quite costly, so a few archaeologists have asked psychics to "read" a photograph or perhaps an object to provide information about the value or location of potential sites.

George McMullen is one psychic who has assisted a number of archaeologists. His abilities were so impressive that one of Canada's best-known archaeologists, J. Norman Emerson, introduced him to members of the Canadian Archaeological Association in 1973. Emerson then went on to announce his own belief in psychic archaeology.

"I'd like some proof," another archaeologist named Jack Miller said. He handed McMullen a small black stone, found on an island off the coast of British Columbia, which had been carved into the shape of a head.

"This carving," McMullen said, after holding the stone for a few moments, "was made by a black man from Haiti who came to Canada as a slave. He was born in West Africa and was sold into slavery in the Caribbean. He was taken from there to Canada on an English ship. Once he reached Canada he escaped and was sheltered by Indians. There he married, raised a family, and died."

Emerson was so skeptical about McMullen's account that he took the carving to many other psychics over the following months. According to author Jeffrey Goodman, they agreed on three facts: the carver was born in Africa, he was taken to America as a slave, and he escaped to British Columbia.

On the surface, this information seems astounding, but consider two other possibilities. Since there is no record of what Emerson said to each psychic, he may have provided some clues that tipped them off to the answers he was seeking. And the stone face itself could have led anyone to the same answer, especially if the face looked African rather than North American.

In his pursuit for evidence, Emerson next asked the Royal Ontario Museum to identify the carved head. Art experts there said it resembled other carvings found in West Africa. Eventually, he received a stronger confirmation from a group of anthropologists who were visiting British Columbia to study the blood types of local Indians. One tribe, they discovered through blood analysis, appeared to have had a black ancestor. Could it have been the man McMullen had described? Emerson believed so, though others were less convinced.

Most psychic archaeologists' claims are much less dramatic than the one made by McMullen. Albert Bowes, a construction worker and gardener who claimed to have ESPower, assisted anthropologist David E. Jones in a series of studies involving psychic archaeology.

Jones first tested Bowes's ESPower with psychometry. An archaeologist friend of Jones selected ten objects, wrapped them in heavy cotton, and placed each in a box. Jones did not know what the ten objects were, so there could be no telepathic communication between him and Bowes. The objects included toy combs from Boston, Massachusetts, manufactured around 1845, and a baseball autographed by J. J. McGraw and Christy Mathewson in 1919.

Of the ten items, Bowes was unable to identify four. Given the fact that these items could have come from any place and any period in the world's history, his ability to identify the remaining six is remarkable. But exactly what did he "see"?

When the box containing the toy combs was placed in front of him, he said:

I kept seeing an object that may have almost been like a comb . . . it could have been like a comb that was in somebody's hair. . . . I kept seeing a woman or a man with long black hair.

Since the combs were completely hidden and didn't rattle in the box, how could Bowes have known it contained combs? Even if he had spoken to the archaeologist who sent the items to Jones, how could he have known that the first box chosen by Jones would contain the combs? If cheating is ruled out, ESP seems a likely explanation.

Or take the autographed baseball. Bowes reported:

> I keep feeling something that would pertain to a game, and I don't know if it's like a ball or . . . like some sort of sport of some kind. I keep seeing somebody talking or little groups of people watching each other.

Although he didn't comment on the autographs, he identified a ball of some sort.

Jones accepted Bowes's work as evidence that he had ESP ability and decided to ask him for information about a site he planned to excavate in east central Florida. He mailed Bowes four photographs of the area and asked him to tape record his psychic impressions about the site within three days. Although Jones admits that Bowes could have taken the photographs to a local museum or college for analysis, the pictures were so "poorly exposed and badly focused" that they revealed no telling details. And the information Bowes gave couldn't have come from experts, unless they had psychic skills.

Bowes was able to identify the location of the site (near water) and describe it (wet and marshy). He also described some people that he "saw" at the site.

> I kept seeing people in gray uniforms or something in a blue or gray uniform and I would say there was something almost . . . they almost looked like cavalry, but I felt they had funny hats. I did feel as though these people could have been someone who . . . I don't know if they captured Indians or whether they made slaves out of them, but I keep seeing chains or shackles and I kept feeling as though this may have caused the people to move. . . . I see them moving and I kept feeling as though they moved south and I don't know if they moved to a place where there was sand, but I kept seeing them moving south. . . .

Jones wondered if the men in uniforms were members of the U.S. Cavalry who escorted mostly Seminole women and children to the Florida Everglades around 1841.

Then Bowes turned his attention to items that he thought the anthropologists would uncover in the site. His short list included a nail fragment and two human skeletons. But Bowes added some interesting information about the remains:

I keep seeing something with a broken neck or something with a . . . I keep feeling the neck. I don't know if someone was hanged or whether there was a problem with someone being attacked but I keep seeing something like their neck was broken.

Remember that Bowes made his observations two months before the excavation began and from a considerable distance. When the team excavated the site, they found just one nail fragment and evidence of only two burials. The second skeleton, only partially complete, was missing its skull.

On the other hand, not everyone was impressed with Bowes's work. For example, archaeologist Kenneth Feder criticized his prediction that the excavation site was near water. Every archaeological site in Florida, wrote Feder, is near water. And Bowes's claim of seeing people in blue uniforms may simply reveal his own knowledge of history rather than a psychic vision.

ESP Use 3: Psychic healing

The possibility of psychic healing — which has been reported throughout history, starting with the ancient Persians, Greeks, and Romans — often causes people to think of miracle cures and "laying on of hands." In reality, psychic healing is probably best called by its most recent name, "therapeutic touch."

Therapeutic touch is a highly structured process. First, the practitioner must be relaxed and concentrate on the patient. Next, the practitioner holds her or his hands a few inches away from the patient's body and moves them over the body looking for a "disturbance." Once the practitioner finds a troublesome place or places, two techniques can be used. Some practitioners actually touch the spot, trying to transfer some of their psychic energy to the patient. Others prefer to hold their hands over the affected area. Whichever technique is used, the practitioner must sense a connection with the patient.

The psychic healer relaxes...

... finds the disturbance ...

...transfers psychic energy to the patient.

What type of results can therapeutic touch produce? Although many people hope to cure terminal illnesses, this seems very unrealistic. Perhaps therapeutic touch can promote *faster* healing. For example, experiments conducted by Dr. Bernard Grad of McGill University in 1960 seemed to suggest this possibility. In the experiments, Dr. Grad inflicted some minor wounds to laboratory mice. Then he asked Oskar Estebany, known for his psychic healing powers, and others who did not claim any psychic healing powers to hold their hands near a cage containing injured mice. Dr. Grad discovered that the mice in Estebany's cage healed faster than the mice in cages Estebany did not try to heal.

I'm healed!

Other experiments have shown that therapeutic touch can reduce a patient's tension and stress levels. Dr. Dolores Krieger, a noted expert in the field, described the case of a teenage girl who had been severely injured in a car accident. The girl was in great pain and could not sleep comfortably. A nurse practiced therapeutic touch with the girl and was able to help her sleep. As the nurse described it in her journal:

95

> [Her] sleep appears more comfortable now. For the first time since she entered the hospital she sleeps peacefully, without twitching, for two uninterrupted hours.

Finally, a few experiments have even suggested that psychic healers may be better at curing minor illnesses than ordinary doctors. For example, in one experiment, a group of thirteen college students suffering from colds were told to visit a local psychic healer. The healer was allowed to say only one thing to the students: "You're healed." Nine of the thirteen students felt better shortly afterward; medical tests confirmed that their colds had improved.

When other doctors from the college's health service heard about this experiment, they were outraged.

"Why didn't you send the students to the health service?" they demanded of the doctor who conducted the experiment. "You'd get the same results if they came here and we told them that they were healed."

So the experiment was repeated, and a different group of students suffering from colds was sent to the health service. The doctors there said, "You're healed."

What were the results this time?

Absolutely none of the students felt better afterward; medical tests confirmed that their colds had not improved. But before you head for a psychic healer the next time you get a cold, keep in mind that this experiment may have been *too* simple. The first group of students knew that the psychic was supposed to heal them, and they may have expected to be cured (which could have sped up their recovery). On the other hand, students in the second group may have been suspicious of doctors who told them that they were healed — without offering any medical attention. Is it surprising that they showed no signs of recovery?

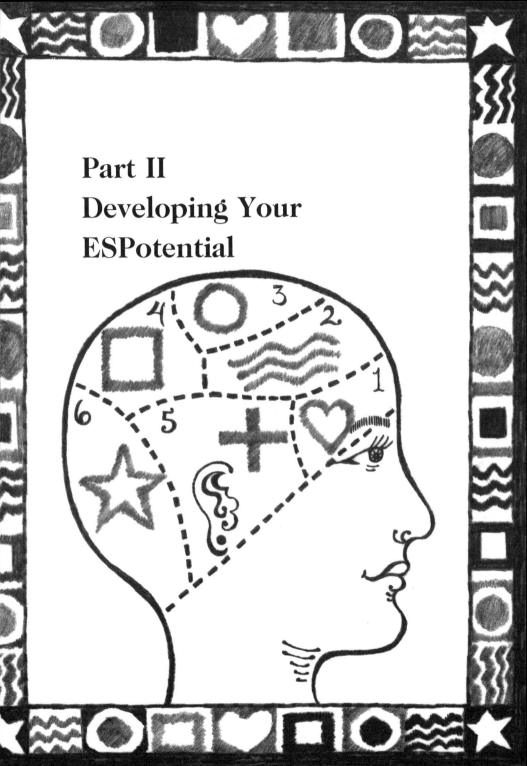

Part II
Developing Your
ESPotential

6. How to Read Your Mother's Mind

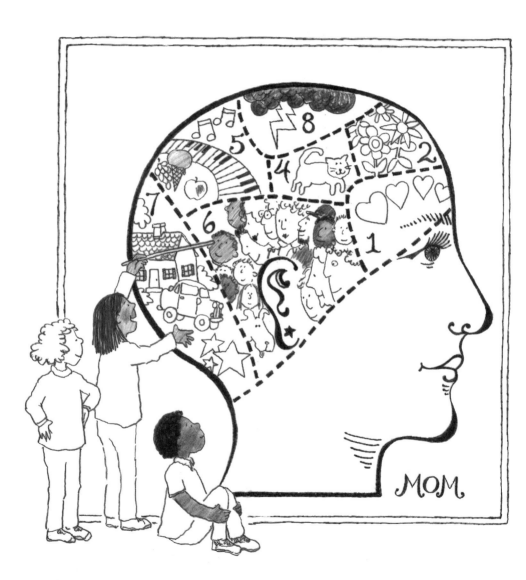

As you know by now, reading your mother's mind is only one part of the ESP process: telepathy. If you have your heart set on having a telepathic experience with your mother, this chapter makes some suggestions to improve your chances. These tips may improve your general ESPotential as well.

ESP Tip 1: Be young

Many parapsychologists believe that children display more ESPotential than adults. This doesn't necessarily mean that children have more psychic ability, but that they have not learned to question (and disbelieve) their experiences. As they grow older, children are taught the rules and laws of the universe and seem to outgrow their extrasensory perception.

Educator and author James W. Peterson believes that most children have the ability to use telepathy with their family members and especially with their parents. Peterson describes the case of a five-year-old boy named Stephen who used telepathy with his parents. As his mother prepared lunch, she might think, *In a minute I must go outside and call Stephen.* Before she could even walk to the door, Stephen would run into the house, asking, "Did you call me just now?"

Stephen also seemed to be aware of every movement his father made with a kind of psychic "tracer beam." This lack of privacy bothered his father because he felt his son was always "watching" him no matter where he went.

One day, on his way home from work, his father decided on the spur of the moment to visit a friend named Joe. As soon as the two men sat down and began to talk, the telephone rang.

It was Stephen.

"Hi, Daddy."

"How did you know where I was? And how in the world did you get Joe's phone number?"

"Daddy," Stephen said, "I 'knew' you were there and I just wanted to say hi."

As you can see, Stephen's psychic gift was not one that pleased his father.

ESP Tip 2: Have previous ESPerience

According to parapsychologists, you are more likely to have a telepathic experience if you've had other ESPeriences. But don't give up if you've never had one; just *believing* in ESP may improve your chances of having an ESPerience — at least in an ESP experiment.

This fact was discovered in a series of experiments conducted first by psychologist Gertrude Schmeidler. In a typical experiment, the participants were asked if they believe in ESP or not. The believers (called sheep) and the nonbelievers (called goats) were then given a standard ESP card test. Schmeidler discovered that sheep repeatedly scored *better* than chance (that is, better than they could have by guessing alone), while goats repeatedly scored *worse* than chance. This seems to mean that goats were working against their ESP ability and deliberately (though without knowing it) selecting the wrong answer. Schmeidler was so surprised by her results that she didn't publish her findings until she had tried the experiment a number of times; each time the results were the same.

So don't despair if you have no previous ESPerience. Becoming a sheep may be enough to provide you with an edge.

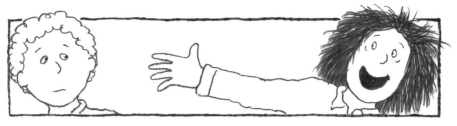

ESP Tip 3: Have an ESPersonality

Do you have an ESPersonality? Psychologists and para-psychologists have found that a number of characteristics seem related to a normal ESPersonality. To see where you stand, look at the following list of personality factors related to high and low scores on ESP tests:

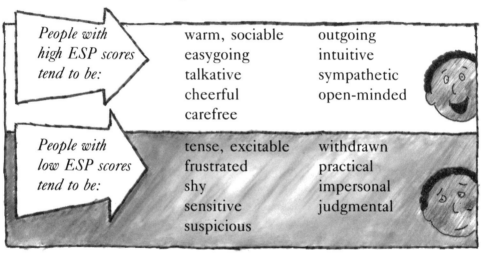

People with high ESP scores tend to be:	warm, sociable	outgoing
	easygoing	intuitive
	talkative	sympathetic
	cheerful	open-minded
	carefree	
People with low ESP scores tend to be:	tense, excitable	withdrawn
	frustrated	practical
	shy	impersonal
	sensitive	judgmental
	suspicious	

If you seem to fit into the second category, don't make plans to change your personality. Parapsychologists are convinced that most people have some ESP ability. So you can still have a telepathic experience even with a "low-ESPersonality."

ESP Tip 4: Pick a good day (or night)

Some days may be better for ESPeriences than others. According to some scientists, geomagnetic activity, weather conditions, and even the moon may have an effect. Although this may seem surprising, research appears to indicate that weather conditions may also effect such things as a person's white blood cell count or even the general suicide rate.

Some scientists — most notably Dr. Michael Persinger of the Neuroscience Laboratory at Canada's Laurentian University — have compared the earth's magnetic field, which can be influenced by solar activity and storms, to the number and type of ESPeriences that have occurred. In general, it appears that telepathy and clairvoyance happen more often on days when geomagnetic activity is quieter than normal. Perhaps high geomagnetic activity interferes with ESP transmission.

The weather may also affect ESPeriences. For example, author D. Scott Rogo described an experiment that took place in 1946 in the Netherlands. The experiment, which involved a psychic trying to roll a certain number on a pair of dice, was not going well. Then a terrible thunderstorm struck. Suddenly, the psychic was able to roll the prearranged number on the dice over and over.

105

Was the result a coincidence or did the thunderstorm increase (at least temporarily) the psychic's powers?

Finally, other researchers suggest that the cycles of the moon may be somewhat related to ESPower. They have found some evidence that dream telepathy may work better on nights when the moon is full, according to author Stanley Krippner.

ESP Tip 5:
Work under the best circumstances

Some scientists believe that telepathy works best in certain situations. Under the most ideal circumstances, the message sender is in some kind of danger, causing adrenaline to rush through her or his body. The message receiver, on the other hand, is in a state of relaxation.

106

Dr. Andrija Puharich, a promoter of this theory, described the case of Jack Sullivan, a welder who was almost suffocated in 1955 when a trench he was working in collapsed around him, burying him in dirt. Sullivan was alone that day. Gasping for air, he realized that his only hope of survival was if a friend checked on him. He thought about his friend Tommy Whittaker, who was working some five miles away. Whittaker immediately sensed that something was wrong at the other site, even though he thought no one was there that day. He quickly went to the site, saw Sullivan's equipment and the collapsed trench, and dug out his friend. His fast work — and the power of telepathy — apparently saved Sullivan's life.

Dr. Puharich claims that the ideal circumstances for telepathy were met in this episode. Sullivan was in danger; Whittaker was relaxed, even though he was working. Sullivan was able to send a strong message; Whittaker was able to receive it.

ESP Tip 6: Relax your mind

According to parapsychologist Charles Honorton, who conducted the ganzfeld study described in Chapter 1, people who meditate or practice other mental relaxation techniques are more likely to pick up ESP information.

By spending quiet time on a regular basis, they have attuned themselves to the inner workings of their minds. When an ESP impression or feeling comes their way, they may have an easier time recognizing it.

If you want to improve your ESPotential, plan to spend some time each day relaxing your mind. If the thought of meditation seems odd, you can try this simple relaxation technique:

> Wearing comfortable clothes, lie down on the floor of your bedroom at a quiet time. Close your eyes and concentrate on how you feel. Don't think about your problems, just relax. To help accomplish this, try some deep breathing: inhale and count to three, then hold your breath for a count of three. Exhale and count to three, then pause and count to three. Keep repeating each step of this exercise — inhale, hold, exhale, pause — counting to three for each step. After repeating it for ten times, you should feel more relaxed.

As you become relaxed, you can try to send someone a message, one she would not be expecting. For example, you might think: "Mom, wear your green dress tomorrow." Concentrate on the message for a minute or two; when your relaxation session is over, write out your message with the date and time you sent it. If your mother happens to wear the green dress the following day, you can immediately show her your message and discuss when she got the idea to wear the dress. Could she have received your message? Or was it just a coincidence?

108

ESP Tip 7: Keep a journal

One of the best ways to tune into your psychic ability is to keep a journal, especially of your dreams. Here's how:

First, plan to write in your journal as soon as you can each morning. In fact, you may be more successful in remembering your dreams if you simply sit up in bed and begin writing. Once you begin the day's activities, you will probably have a hard time recalling what you dreamed.

Second, add other ESPeriences that occur during your waking hours to your journal at the end of the day. This way you will be better able to prove that you've had a precognitive vision or a series of telepathic encounters with your mother.

Finally, whether you keep a journal or not, tell someone if you believe that you've had a dream involving ESP. You should do this right away, in order to prove *when* you had your dream. Otherwise, no one will believe your claim is true.

For example, a four-year-old boy named Craig woke up screaming from a dream on the morning of November 18, 1950. His father comforted him until Craig was calm. Then he told his father about his dream:

I dreamed you were in the water, Daddy. There was tall grass all around, and you were in the water. I called and called to you and you kept trying to come out of the water to me.

Craig's father listened to the dream, but, as most parents might, didn't believe that it was important and put it out of his mind.

Two days later, a tragic incident renewed the memory of Craig's dream and left an impression that his father would never forget. Craig's father and his father's brother went duck hunting and spent most of the day sitting in a duck blind behind some tall reeds. Shortly before they planned to leave for home, they shot two ducks, which fell into the lake. They climbed into their boat to get the ducks, but high winds and strong waves forced the boat further into the lake, where it capsized.

Although Craig's uncle drowned, his father managed to swim ashore in the choppy water.

"The thought of Craig's dream was before me the entire time," he later reported.

ESP Tip 8: Control your expectations

Although you are probably interested in ESPossibilities, guard against expecting too much. Don't spend time hoping to have a precognitive experience or to receive a telepathic message — ESP doesn't happen because a person *wants* it to happen.

Even if you follow all eight suggestions, you may not be able to read your mother's mind or have an ESPerience. Keep in mind that ESP happens unexpectedly to most people — and you may not even be aware of it when it does occur.

Parapsychologist Martin Johnson conducted an interesting experiment a number of years ago. A college psychology professor, he decided to test his students in a slightly different way. On the day of a scheduled exam, he handed each student a two-page test with eight short-answer questions. The first page was taped onto the front of a manila envelope; the second page was taped onto the back of the same envelope. The students did not know what was inside the envelope, since it was sealed.

They were told to take the test as usual. Inside the envelope were the correct answers to half of the questions on the exam. It was impossible to see through the envelope, and it couldn't be opened. Johnson wanted to find out whether the students would perform better on the questions to which he had provided the answers.

Johnson varied the answers that he provided. For example, one student's envelope might have contained the answers to questions 1, 3, 5, and 8, while another student's envelope contained the answers to 2, 4, 5, and

MARTIN JOHNSON'S ESP EXPERIMENT

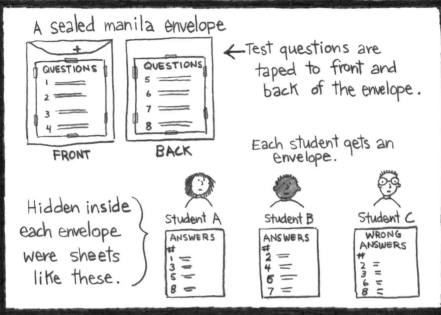

A sealed manila envelope

QUESTIONS
1 ___
2 ___
3 ___
4 ___

FRONT

QUESTIONS
5 ___
6 ___
7 ___
8 ___

BACK

← Test questions are taped to front and back of the envelope.

Each student gets an envelope.

Hidden inside each envelope were sheets like these.

Student A

ANSWERS
#
1 ___
3 ___
5 ___
8 ___

Student B

ANSWERS
#
2 ___
4 ___
6 ___
7 ___

Student C

WRONG ANSWERS
#
2 ___
3 ___
6 ___
8 ___

7. Johnson hired outside scorers to judge how closely a student's answers matched the "target" answers in the envelope. He reported the results this way: "The unseen answers seemed to influence the quality of [the students'] answers." This implies that although they did not write answers exactly as they were recorded inside the envelope, the students appeared to have written better answers when information was provided. What is most interesting is the idea that the students appeared to be using ESP without knowing it.

The next time one of your teachers gives an exam, explain that you'd like to try an experiment involving

ESP. You can then describe Johnson's experiment and hope, if your teacher agrees, that your ESPower allows you to find the information inside the envelope. Beware, though, if your teacher should decide to make a slight change in the experiment, as Johnson did. In one round, he deliberately put the *wrong* answers to half of the questions in the envelope. The students used that incorrect information much more than luck alone (and bad luck at that) would have predicted. The hidden incorrect answers seemed to influence the students' own answers; they scored poorly on the exam as a result.

7. Experimenting with ESPower

Now you're ready to participate in some experiments designed to help measure your ESPower. Almost all present-day parapsychologists conduct experiments to prove some aspect of ESP. When they do, they try to follow three basic guidelines, according to authors Hans Eysenck and Carl Sargent:

1. Conduct the experiment in a quiet, controlled setting. ESP experiments work best when outside noises and distractions are eliminated or at least reduced. Make sure that no one will interrupt you once the experiment begins.

2. Avoid giving any clues. Many ESP experiments have failed because the experimenter provided clues, usually unconsciously, to the persons taking part in the study. To avoid giving clues, there are three steps you should follow. First, use only new materials. For example, old cards may have bent corners that are easy to identify. Second, make sure the materials have not been arranged in a set pattern. Scientists prefer "random order." That's why cards in an ESP experiment are shuffled and cut, so no one (not even the experimenter) knows the order in which the cards will appear. Finally, if you repeat the experiment, follow the same procedures each time. For example, if you give verbal directions, repeat the exact wording each time. Otherwise, you might supply some unintentional clue.

3. Record the results accurately. Changing the results to make them look better doesn't help the study of ESP. Whatever happens, record exactly what happens even if this shows that no ESP was detected.

How will you perform on the following experiments? Since everyone is born with different amounts of ES-Potential, don't worry whether you're the Michelangelo or Mickey Mouse of ESP. Rather, concentrate on understanding the methods and analyzing the results of these practical experiments. And remember: even with zero ESPower, you can become an excellent parapsychologist.

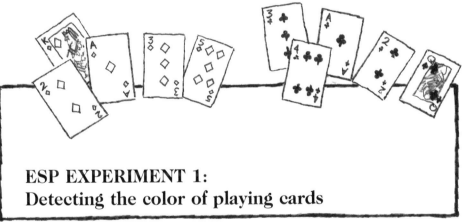

ESP EXPERIMENT 1:
Detecting the color of playing cards

The simplest ESP experiment can be done with a pack of playing cards. Remove five black cards and five red cards from the deck, preferably from the same suits, and put the remaining cards away.

To test clairvoyance: Shuffle the ten cards well, cut them once or twice, and place the stack on the table in front of you. Concentrate on the top card and decide whether it is black or red. Write your answer on a recording form, as shown on page 121. Pick up the card and, without looking at it, place it in a separate pile. Even if you realize that the tenth card should be black (that is, if you've "seen" five red cards and only four black ones), try to "see" it because you may have made an error or two on the earlier cards.

When you are finished with all ten cards, turn the discard pile face up and check your results.

To test precognition: Do not shuffle the cards. Sit down and look at a clock. Tell yourself: "Ten minutes from now I am going to shuffle and cut the cards two times. In what order will the colors appear?" Then record your predictions on the recording form.

At the chosen time, shuffle and cut the cards. Then turn them face up one at a time, comparing your predictions on the recording form.

To test telepathy: You must work with a companion (the receiver) who should be seated looking away from you. Shuffle and cut the cards. Then say to the receiver: "I'm picking up a card now." Remove the top card from the stack, look at its color, and concentrate on transmitting this information to the receiver. Think *black, black, black* or *red, red, red* for ten seconds or so. Then say, "Record the color you think I sent." After the receiver has written her or his guess on the recording form, place the card you sent face down in a separate pile. Repeat these steps until you have run through the stack.

When you have transmitted all ten cards, compare the receiver's recording form and the discard pile to check the results.

Scoring your experiment: Regardless of which ESPossibility you test, guessing alone should allow you to get five correct answers out of ten. (After all, this is like taking a true/false test; with only two choices, you have a fifty percent chance of getting the right answer.) If you consistently score seven correct answers or better, you are tuned into your ESP. If you consistently score three correct answers or fewer, you are subconsciously tuning out your ESP and working to counteract it (are you a goat, by any chance?).

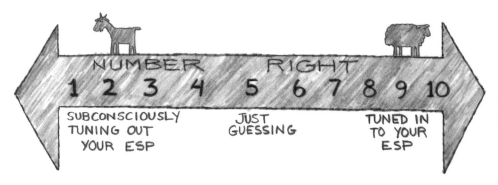

NUMBER RIGHT

1 2 3 4 5 6 7 8 9 10

SUBCONSCIOUSLY TUNING OUT YOUR ESP   JUST GUESSING   TUNED IN TO YOUR ESP

VARIATIONS WITH PLAYING CARDS

If you score well on one or more of these experiments, you can advance to a more complicated ESP experiment. Use a regular deck of cards with the jokers removed. Then, rather than sending or predicting the *color* of each card, guess the *identity* of the card (for example, "Jack of Spades"). Anyone should be able to guess one of the 52 cards correctly. If you predict three, four, or more (the more you hit, the better) correctly, the experiment may provide proof that you have ESP.

ESP EXPERIMENT 1 RECORDING FORM

CARD GUESS: R = Red
               B = Black

ACCURACY: ✓ = correct

1 _____

2 _____

3 _____

4 _____

5 _____

6 _____

7 _____

8 _____

9 _____

10 _____

ESP EXPERIMENT 2:
Detecting symbols of ESP cards

Regular playing cards were never intended to test ESP and caused many complications during experiments. For example, trying to guess the identity of 52 *different* cards was downright discouraging. Even if a participant scored five hits, he or she still managed to identify forty-seven cards incorrectly. So J. B. Rhine, parapsychologist and husband of Louisa Rhine, and his associate Karl Zener tried to create a more appropriate set of cards with fewer symbols. The card deck they developed, known as Zener cards, contains five symbols: a star, a circle, a cross, a square, and three wavy lines.

All of the symbols are repeated five times in the deck, for a total of twenty-five cards. You may be able to buy a pack of Zener cards at a local bookstore, especially if it specializes in New Age material. If you can't find a deck, you can make your own. Here's how:

1. Get twenty-five new index cards. Do not mix old and new cards; otherwise, you may be giving clues as to the identities of the cards.

2. Draw each of the Zener symbols on five cards. Try to make each of the symbols identical. You may even want to create a stencil for each symbol and use a black marker to fill it in. Make sure, however, that your marker does not "bleed" through the card in order to avoid giving any clues to the symbol.

Or you could copy or trace this page.
Cut out and glue to index cards.

Now that you have a set of ESP cards, you can continue to test your ESP with the following experiment, which is described in a more scientific format. As you practice these experiments with your family and friends, notice that the person participating in an experiment is referred to as the *subject,* a term commonly used by scientists and researchers.

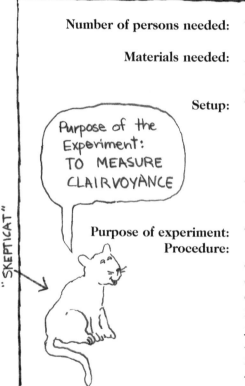

Number of persons needed: Two (the subject and the experimenter)

Materials needed: A deck of ESP cards, a screen (made from a cardboard box), recording form, and pencil

Setup: The experimenter and subject should sit across from each other at a table or desk. They should be separated by a small screen so that the subject cannot see the cards. This makes sure that the subject does not get any visual clues about the cards.

Purpose of experiment: To measure clairvoyance

Procedure:
1. The experimenter shuffles the cards and places them face down on the table, so that the subject cannot see them.
2. The experimenter asks the subject: *What is the top card?*
3. The subject calls out the card's name.
4. The experimenter records the name on the recording form.

EXPERIMENTER

What is the top card?

SUBJECT

Ace of clubs.

5. The experimenter places the card face down in another pile without looking at it. Repeat steps 2 through 5 until the subject has named each card.

Checking the results: Determine the number of hits and misses by comparing the discarded cards to the results on the recording form. Then the cards can be reshuffled, and the experimenter can conduct another run.

Determining the subject's success: A subject using ESP cards should score five correct answers by chance alone. A subject who identifies ten or more cards is probably showing some clairvoyance. A subject with true clairvoyance will also be able to score well during a series of runs through the deck.

ESP EXPERIMENT 2 RECORDING FORM

CARD   GUESS (○□☆※+)   ACCURACY: ✓ = correct

1 _____

2 _____

3 _____

4 _____

5 _____

6 _____

7 _____

8 _____

9 _____

10 _____

11 _____

12 _____

13 _____

14 _____

15 _____

16 _____

17 _____

18 _____

19 _____

20 _____

21 _____

22 _____

23 _____

24 _____

25 _____

VARIATIONS WITH ESP CARDS

To test telepathy: Seat two subjects (a sender and a receiver) in adjacent rooms separated by a closed door. They should not be in communication with each other. The sender should have a picture of the five Zener symbols. Both sender and receiver should have a recording form. Tell the sender to visualize one symbol and transmit it to the receiver for 30 seconds. [In this way, the sender can use only telepathy (not clairvoyance) to communicate to the receiver. If the sender looked at a Zener card or wrote the name of the symbol down before sending it to the receiver, the experimenter would not know if the receiver used clairvoyance or telepathy.] Tell the receiver to be aware of any symbol that appears in her or his mind. At the end of thirty seconds, ask the receiver to record any symbol visualized. Then ask the sender to record the symbol transmitted. (By recording the image first, the receiver cannot use clairvoyance to see what the sender recorded.) The sender should transmit at least twenty-five symbols per session so that success can be determined accurately. A score of five should be achieved through guessing alone. The higher the score, the more likely telepathy has taken place.

127

ESP EXPERIMENT 3: Using telephone telepathy or caller clairvoyance

Parapsychologists have criticized ESP card experiments as being too routine and impersonal to test ESP; they believe that ESP should be measured in more interesting ways. You can easily devise a test of your ESPower with your telephone. When the phone rings, try to identify who's calling before you answer. Here's an example:

One day when your phone rings, you think: *Grandma is calling.*

"Hello?" you say.

"Hi, honey," the voice says. "It's Grandma. What have you been up to?"

You could have known that your grandmother was calling for at least four reasons: this could be the usual time that she calls; she may have said that she would call sometime that day; you could have been lucky; you have ESPower.

If ESPower was involved, you may wonder if you used clairvoyance or telepathy to identify her. Did you see an image of her in your mind (clairvoyance) or did you have mind-to-mind contact (telepathy)? Because this is often difficult to determine, be content with your GESPower.

If you want to be more scientific in your telephone telepathy experiments, take the following steps:

Number of persons needed:	One (you)
Materials needed:	Recording form, pencil, and a clock
Setup:	Keep your recording form and pencil by the telephone.
Purpose of experiment:	To measure GESP.
Procedure:	1. When the phone rings, write down your first idea of who is calling *before you answer the phone.* To make sure you have time to record your prediction and answer the phone, you might want to develop a list of abbreviations (GM = grandma; M = Mom, etc.).
	2. After you answer the phone, record the name of the actual caller and the time of the phone call.
Checking the results:	On a regular basis (either every day or every week), tally the number of hits you've made.

Purpose of the experiment: TO MEASURE GESP

Grandma!

Determining the subject's success: Repeated hits are a sign of general ESP, although many will say that you were simply making a lucky guess. Repeated hits with the same person are perhaps a better sign. You may be able to identify one specific caller better than others because you have a telepathic connection with that person. Or you may simply be shrewd enough to predict a person who calls your home often.

Date: July 7			
Time	Prediction	Real Person	Accuracy
8:12 p.m.	GM	Grandma	X
8:35 p.m.	sister	someone for Mom	
8:50 p.m.	P	Ellen's mother	
9:03 p.m.	P	Patty	X

DING ♪
DONG

I bet my sister's at the door...

DING
DONG ♫

VARIATIONS ON
TELEPHONE TELEPATHY

You can apply what you know about telephone telepathy to another common situation: doorbell dilemma. Whenever the doorbell rings, try to know who is at the door before you answer it. Again, make sure you record your prediction before you open the door.

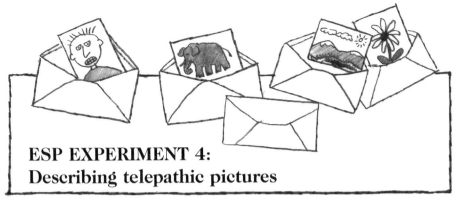

ESP EXPERIMENT 4:
Describing telepathic pictures

Telepathic picture experiments are another way to make an ESP test more interesting. Before you can conduct the experiment, however, you will need to find ten pictures (photographs, drawings, advertisements) from magazines or other sources. Use three factors in selecting the pictures:

1. Use clear pictures that do not have writing or illustrations on the other side, since this may be distracting. Postcards or notecards are suitable for this. You may also use photographs that you or others have taken.

2. Vary the type of images. Some could be landscapes (a beautiful sunset, a photograph of a beach) but others should display emotional or disturbing content (a child crying, an angry man).

3. Place each picture in a separate opaque (see-proof) envelope of the same size. The envelopes should be new and have no noticeable markings on them. By putting the pictures in envelopes, you will make sure that no one (not even the experimenter) knows which picture is being tested. This rules out telepathic communication between the experimenter and the receiver.

131

Sender   Experimenter   *shuffle the envelopes and choose one.*   *When I leave, open the envelope and remove the picture. Then concentrate on transmitting the image to the receiver. I'll give you 60 seconds. When I knock on the door, seal the picture back in the envelope.*

Number of persons needed:	Two subjects (the sender and the receiver) and the experimenter
Materials needed:	Ten envelopes (each containing a different picture), recording paper and pencil, and a watch with a second hand for the experimenter
Setup:	Needed are two adjacent rooms separated by a door — one for the sender and one for the receiver.
Purpose of experiment:	To measure telepathy
Procedure:	1. The experimenter says to the sender: *Shuffle the envelopes and choose one.*

Purpose of the experiment: TO MEASURE TELEPATHY

"SKEPTICAT"

2. The experimenter says to the sender: *When I leave the room, open the envelope and remove the picture. Then concentrate on transmitting the image of the picture to the receiver in the next room. I will give you sixty seconds to do this. When I knock on the door, put the picture back in the envelope and seal it.*

3. The experimenter notes the time, leaves the sender's room, and goes into the receiver's room. The experimenter says: *Sit very still and draw or write about any images that appear in your mind during the next minute or so. I'll tell you when to stop.*

Experimenter

Sit very still and draw or write about any images that appear in your mind during the next minute or so. I'll tell you when to stop.

Receiver

4. The experimenter stops the sender and the receiver at the designated time. Then the experimenter collects the first envelope from the sender and the drawing/writing from the receiver. The experimenter should number the envelope and picture so that they can be matched later.

5. The experimenter asks the sender to select another envelope. Repeat until the sender has used all ten pictures.

Checking the results: The experimenter should compare the receiver's drawings or descriptions to the sender's pictures.

Determining the subject's success: Some judgment should be used in deciding whether telepathy was involved. As long as there was no verbal communication between the sender and receiver during the experiment, figure that any similarity between the drawing/description and the picture are the result of telepathy. If telepathic communication is taking place, it should be detected on a number (though not necessarily all) of the pictures.

VARIATIONS ON
TELEPATHIC PICTURES

You can improve the experiment by adopting the ganzfeld procedure (described in Chapter 1). Provide a couch or bed for the receiver. Place halved Ping-Pong balls (stuffed with cotton) on her or his eyes. If possible, position a lamp with a red bulb above the receiver's head, so that pinkish light will filter through. Block out all outside noises and distractions. If possible, place headphones on the receiver and play a blank tape. Finally, use a deep breathing exercise (see page 108) to help the receiver relax before the experiment begins. As the sender begins to transmit the image, ask the receiver to say out loud whatever images appear; tape record the session. Then compare the spoken images to the picture the sender transmitted.

ESP Experiment 5: Remote viewing

One much more energetic ESP experiment involves what is called remote viewing. This is basically an experiment in telepathy. The sender visits a site and tries to send information about the location to the receiver back in the experimenter's room.

To conduct a remote-viewing experiment, select ten places that are located within walking distance. Write each place on an index card (along with directions for finding it, if necessary). Then put each index card in an opaque envelope.

Number of persons needed:	Two subjects (the sender and the receiver) and the experimenter
Materials needed:	Ten unnumbered, unmarked envelopes (each containing a different location), recording paper and pencil, and synchronized watches for the sender and the experimenter

continued next page →

Setup: One room for the receiver and ten nearby locations for the sender

Purpose of experiment: To measure telepathy

Procedure:

1. The experimenter says to the sender: *Shuffle the envelopes and choose one. When I leave, open the envelope and read the index card. It will have a nearby location printed on it. Fifteen minutes from now you should be at that location. At that time, concentrate on transmitting the scene that you are looking at to the receiver in the next room. I will give you ten minutes to do this. Then come back here. Let's synchronize our watches.*

3. The sender leaves. A few minutes before the designated time, the experimenter tells the receiver: *Sit very still and draw or write about any images that appear in your mind during the next ten minutes. I'll tell you when to stop.*

4. The experimenter stops the receiver at the designated time. Then the experimenter collects the drawing/writing from the receiver and, when the sender returns, the index card stating the location.

5. The experimenter asks the sender what he or she saw at the location. If possible, record this on tape.

6. The experimenter asks the sender to select another envelope. Repeat until the sender has used all ten pictures (or until the sender is too tired to continue).

Checking the results:	The experimenter should compare the receiver's drawing/description to the sender's description of the location.
Determining the subject's success:	Any similarities suggest that telepathy was taking place. If the telepathy is strong, the experimenter should find many similarities over a number of remote viewings.

In one actual remote-viewing experiment, researcher Tom Dempsey described what happened when Mike (the sender) went to a location and tried to transmit information about it to Linda (the receiver). Linda told Dempsey (the experimenter) that she had impressions of people moving. One person was wearing tennis shoes and another had a yellow baseball hat. She saw Mike looking through a big window. Finally, she saw a building, perhaps made of cinder blocks.

When Mike returned, he told Dempsey that he had selected a card that told him to go to an auto painting shop. The building was made of cinder blocks and had several large windows that he had looked through. As he observed the building, two boys stood outside. One was wearing a red baseball hat and tennis shoes. These similarities were striking and suggested that telepathy had taken place. What's more, when Linda was taken to the building later, she pointed to the spot where Mike had parked his car.

See if you can match Dempsey's results.

ESP EXPERIMENT 6: Knowing the headlines

One experiment that psychic Alan Vaughan uses to test himself involves browsing through the newspaper headlines — only he "reads" the edition that will be published tomorrow (or even next week). Although he hasn't had great success with this (after all, no one can foresee tomorrow's headlines very often or very clearly), he has had some.

For example, on January 10, 1981, he tried to predict information that might appear in the January 24th edition of the *Los Angeles Times*. One of his predictions involved a large photograph that showed an injured man climbing down a fire ladder from a high place. Vaughan saw the photograph so clearly that he was able to say, "The fire ladder is shown at an angle on the right side of the photo." Although no such photograph appeared

on January 24th, one did on January 29th. The caption read:

Fire Captain Mike Reagan grimaces in pain after he and Fireman Burton E. Sander, legs tangled in ladder, fell from the facade of a North Hollywood restaurant while fighting the blaze. Eight firefighters were injured and one died when the roof collapsed. Story on page 3.

When Vaughan turned to page three, he saw another photo which showed "two firefighters on the roof and a ladder at an angle on the right side of the photo."

139

What do you think? Did precognition occur — even if he missed the target date by five days? Or was it simply a coincidence?

Number of persons needed:	One (you)
Materials needed:	Recording paper and pencil
Setup:	Station yourself in a quiet room where you can relax and where you will not be disturbed.
Purpose of experiment:	To measure precognition
Procedure:	1. Select a date sometime in the near future. This will be the date for which you will predict headlines in your local newspaper.

2. Sit down and relax. Then try to visualize what the front page of the newspaper will look like on that date. You may see a photograph first. As you get an impression, write it down (or tape record it, if you will be distracted by writing). Don't worry about what it means, simply record it. Try to see the headline of the main story. Record anything you see. After you have spent ten minutes visualizing the newspaper, stop. If you have tape recorded your impressions, transcribe the tape now. Put your notes away.

Checking the results: Every day, check the predictions that you made and compare them with the information carried in your paper.

Determining the subject's success: You may miss the date; you may also miss the page the information appears on. But you will be able to detect any similarities to your predictions. Simply make sure that your predictions aren't too easy (during an election campaign, for example, a prediction that one candidate's name will appear on the front page is guaranteed to be correct — but this doesn't mean you've had a precognitive experience).

8. Becoming an ESPrivate Eye

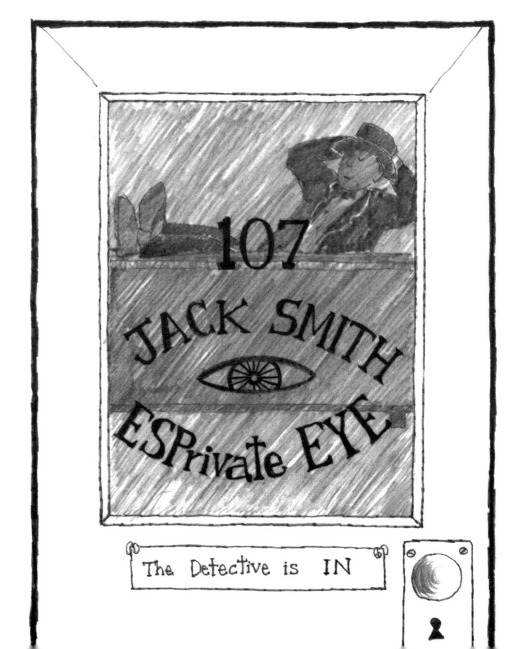

Even if you don't discover much ESPower within yourself, you can still specialize in ESP investigations. You'll want to consider two types of exploration:

ESP Investigation 1: Analyzing ESP stories

One way of doing further work on ESP is to read and analyze true stories involving ESP. If this sounds too easy, think again. Reading an ESP story *is* easy, but deciding whether the story could possibly be true is much more difficult.

Reread the following ESP account, which was used earlier in this book:

A pilot was practicing some difficult maneuvers in her Piper Cub one day in 1956. Suddenly she felt that something was wrong — not with the airplane but on the ground. She doubted this strange feeling, though, and pushed it from her mind and continued to practice. But the feeling kept returning, each time breaking her concentration.

Finally, she stopped practice and gave in to the feeling. She flew seventy miles off her intended course and noticed a car that had gone off a deserted country road. Without hesitating, she landed the small plane on the road and ran to the car. There, she pulled an unconscious woman from behind the wheel.

As she dragged the woman away from the car, the gas tank exploded and the car burst into flames. She laid the woman on the ground, only then realizing that the woman was her mother.

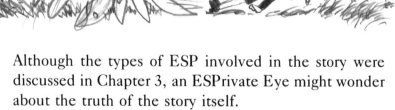

Although the types of ESP involved in the story were discussed in Chapter 3, an ESPrivate Eye might wonder about the truth of the story itself.

Use this form to determine the truth:

ESPrivate Eye Analysis Form

SOURCE:

Where did the story come from? _____

_____

_____

Can you find the original story?

_____

EVENT: Does the story report the
names of people involved? _____

_____

_____

... the precise location of the incident? _____

_____

...the specific date of the events? _____

REPORT: Who reported the incident? _____

When was the report made? _____

Could there be any errors in the report? _____

_____

_____

_____

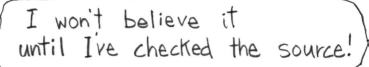

I won't believe it until I've checked the source!

1. Source of material.   Where did the story come from? Although the story about the pilot was used by Bernard Gittelson in his book *Intangible Evidence,* he never mentions where he found it. Did he know the pilot personally? Or did she write him about the incident? Or, most likely, did he find it in a book or magazine? If so, where? An ESPrivate Eye should always be able to check the source of a story, especially one as remarkable as this.

2. Identity of person, place, and date.   Another way to judge the truth of an ESP story is the type of information the author presents. In this case, the pilot's name, the location (for example, what state did this happen in? or did this happen in another country?), and the exact date are not given. This lack of specific information doesn't mean that the story is false, but checking its accuracy would be difficult. By knowing when and where this incident took place, an ESPrivate Eye would be able to read a local newspaper to see if a woman had been injured in a car accident (and perhaps rescued by her pilot daughter). Even if the clairvoyant part of the case wasn't reported, such a dramatic event should have received some type of newspaper coverage.

I won't believe it until I've checked the specific information!

I won't believe it until I know if the report is accurate!

3. *Type and date of ESP report.* If the incident happened in 1956, how and when did the woman report the events? Did she immediately write a journal entry describing the events in detail? Did Gittelson or a newspaper reporter interview the woman shortly after the incident? Or did the woman write about her experience years after it happened? If so, her memory may not have captured the true events of that day. An ESPrivate Eye will want to determine if the report could contain any errors.

INVESTIGATION SUGGESTION

Reread the stories reported in this book. Now that you have a way to analyze them, apply the ESPrivate Eye Analysis Form to each one. Then judge the truth for yourself.

ESP Investigation 2:
Documenting ESP experiences

If you want to move beyond questioning ESP stories you read in books, you may be able to document an actual ESP case.

Imagine that your friend Stacy says one day:

"The most incredible thing happened last week. I was walking home from school when all of a sudden my mom drove up in the car and asked, 'Are you all right?' I no sooner stepped off the sidewalk and walked toward the car when the sidewalk collapsed. If I had been standing there, I really would've gotten hurt. But the weird thing is that my mom knew I was going to be hurt. That's why she came to find me."

You believe Stacy but you want to prove that her story is true. Here are the steps an ESPrivate Eye would follow:

STEPS TO VERIFY AN ESP STORY

1. Ask her to write a complete report of the experience. It's important that she stick to the facts and not write what she thinks happened to her mother. She should record only what she *knows*.

2. Ask Stacy's mother to write a report of the experience. Again, she should record what happened to her.

3. Ask other friends and family members who know about the ESPerience to write a statement that indicates when they heard about it.

4. Look for contradictions in the stories. If you find any, you should question the persons to clarify any conflicting details.

5. Interview a person in the city department responsible for repairing sidewalks and write a report of the interview, including the date and time. The main purpose of this step is to discover when the sidewalk at the location of the ESPerience collapsed. Does the time of the collapse match Stacy's and her mother's accounts?

6. Write a brief summary of the information and, if you conclude that ESP was involved, send it to a research organization, such as the American Society for Psychical Research (5 West 73rd Street, New York, N.Y. 10023).

Dr. Ian Stevenson, who has investigated many unusual incidents, wrote about an ESPerience that occurred to the Judd family of Upland, California, in his book *Telepathic Impressions*.

Around 10:00 A.M. on Tuesday, December 18, 1967, Mrs. Brigitte Judd was all set to have a quick cup of coffee at the apartment of her next-door neighbor. She left Cindy, her nine-year-old daughter, to watch younger brother John and four-year-old sister Celeste. Then she hurried next door.

Ten minutes later, John ran into the neighbor's apartment.

"Puppy bit Dumpling!" he screamed.

Puppy was the name of the family's dachshund, and Dumpling was Celeste's nickname. Brigitte ran home where she found Celeste screaming. Puppy was skulking in a corner nearby.

Brigitte described what happened next in a letter written January 9, 1968, to Dr. Stevenson:

> Naturally I was upset. My four-year-old . . . played with the dog all the time. Now the dog had bitten her! I first calmed [Celeste] down and determined that the "bite" was mostly a large bruise on her mouth that slowly turned dark blue. There were only her own teethmarks on the inside of her lip. The two older children confirmed that the dog had growled and snapped at her though. All this time I thought strongly of my husband and what he would say or do.

At 10:30 that morning, the telephone rang. It was Mr. Judd.

"What's wrong?" he asked. "I know something has happened. Tell me, what's going on?"

"Oh, nothing," Brigitte said. "Puppy just bit Dumpling, that's all."

Brigitte was surprised that her husband had somehow found out about the incident. But she was even more surprised to discover that he was about one hundred miles from home, on his way back to the office from a business call, when he realized something was wrong.

When Dr. Stevenson received Mrs. Judd's letter, he didn't just file it away. He wrote to Mr. Judd, asking him to write his own account. Mr. Judd wrote that he had driven from Los Angeles to San Diego that morning to make a business call. On his return, he felt uneasy.

He put it this way:

I became more and more worried over nothing in particular. When I reached the office, I could contain myself no longer and I called home. The only thing I could think to say to my wife was, "What's going on?"

Again, Stevenson was not satisfied. He wanted to know more of the details of the case. In particular, he wanted to know if Mr. Judd had a habit of calling home regularly. If he did, the timing of his phone call may simply have been a coincidence. He wrote another letter to the Judds.

Mrs. Judd replied that her husband rarely called home, because it was a long-distance call. "I can tell you," she wrote, "that my husband has not called me more than five or six times during the last year."

Before finishing his investigation, Stevenson interviewed the Judds at home because he believed that the case had "borderline significance" — meaning that ESP was probably involved but in a commonplace way. Only then, when he had all the facts, did Stevenson (like any ESPrivate Eye) write about the Judds and their experience.

9. Two Intuitive Investigations

Cases involving psychic criminology are often the most fascinating and frustrating. Here are two investigations that were conducted more than one hundred years apart. Though both are still officially unsolved, you may draw your own conclusions about the perpetrators as well as the psychic nature of the investigations.

One of the most famous examples of psychic criminology involved an investigation done by Robert James Lees in London in the late 1880s. Lees, a psychic who had clairvoyant visions, was well known at that time because he had worked as a journalist and had written a number of books concerning psychic power. He was respected by many, including Queen Victoria, who supposedly asked him for occasional readings.

155

But today his greatest claim to fame is his involvement in one of the most brutal and sensational murder cases in history: the killings done by Jack the Ripper.

On August 7, 1888, the first of a series of young women was brutally murdered in London's East End. The police had no leads, though they suspected a doctor must be responsible for the murders, given the surgical precision of the injuries.

Where did Robert James Lees come into the investigation? The night of September 6, almost a week after a second murder, he had a clairvoyant vision of a man and woman walking by a bar at night. Lees's vision was so clear that he even saw the time on a clock that hung behind the bar: 12:40 A.M. Then he was stunned, as the vision continued with the man murdering the woman.

He went to Scotland Yard the next day, where he was greeted as a crank.

"When do you think this murder will take place?" the sergeant on duty asked him.

"Tomorrow night," he said.

In fact, Jack the Ripper struck the following night. When he learned of the murder, Lees visited the murder site and recognized the scene he had envisioned. He was so disturbed by living out his vision that he left London with his family and headed for Europe. The vision "made such an impression on me that my whole nervous system was seriously shaken," he later reported.

Because he had no further visions on his European trip, he decided to return home. But shortly after his return, he and his wife were riding a bus when he noticed the man from his vision. Lees took a good look at him and then nudged his wife.

"That man is Jack the Ripper," he said.

When the man rose to get off, Lees did, too.

"I'm going to follow him," he told his wife. "I'll be home soon."

Although she tried to argue with him, Lees continued to follow the man as he walked across London.

At one point, Lees saw a police officer.

"Look there," Lees said, pointing to the man. "That's Jack the Ripper. I demand that you take him into custody."

The officer, convinced that Lees was crazy, laughed at him.

"I'm telling you the truth," Lees said.

"I'll take you in if you don't get on your way and stop all this nonsense," the officer warned.

By now, the man had stopped a cab and driven away.

Later that night, Lees had another psychic impression, though it wasn't as vivid as his first vision. But he could see the face of the victim and the disturbing fact that her ears had been removed.

Again he went to Scotland Yard, where he was scoffed at — until he mentioned what he had noticed about the ears. They had just received a letter supposedly written by Jack the Ripper in which he said that the next time he would "clip the lady's ears off."

The next night, September 30, he struck twice. The first victim had her ears severed. When Lees heard the news, he collapsed.

A few nights later, he felt strong enough to go out to dinner with two friends when he had his third — and final — vision.

"Jack the Ripper has committed another murder!" he told them. According to some accounts, he hurried to

158

the police, who asked him to visit the crime scene and possibly pick up some clues. From there he led detectives through the streets of London to the West End. He finally stopped in front of a large house.

"Inside there is the murderer — the man you are looking for," he told them.

"Impossible," the chief inspector said, for the house belonged to a well-known doctor, Sir William Gull.

"I'm telling you the truth," Lees said.

"Then give me some information. If this is the Ripper's house and I ring the bell, what will I see when the door opens? If you truly have second sight, I'll go after the doctor."

Lees told him that there would be a black chair on the right, a stained glass window at the far end, and a bullmastiff sleeping at the foot of the stairs.

The maid answered the bell. The inspector saw the chair and the stained glass window, but no dog.

"Is there a dog in the house?"

"Why no, sir," the maid said. "I just let him out in the back garden."

Only then did the inspector ask to speak to the doctor's wife.

"Madam, I'm here to inquire about your husband."

With that introduction, he led the conversation to uncover a number of interesting facts about Sir William Gull. He seemed to have two ways of behaving. Most of the time he was kind and thoughtful; but on rare occasions, his wife had known him to be cruel and almost evil. Once she had found him torturing the family cat. Another time he had beaten his young son. Finally, he had taken to disappearing — on evenings that seemed to coincide with the nights that the Ripper murdered his victims.

At that point in their conversation, Sir William came downstairs and allowed himself to be questioned. He told the inspector that he had occasional memory losses. After one, he found blood on his shirt. After another he had scratches on his face. When the inspector asked to examine the doctor's wardrobe, he discovered a tweed suit and overcoat, similar to the ones that Jack the Ripper had worn, according to the testimony of a few eyewitnesses.

By the next day, November 9, 1888, Sir William had been committed to an asylum. Since Jack the Ripper murdered no more after that, Lees believed that his encounters (psychic and otherwise) with Gull proved that he was the Ripper. Of course, many other theories about the Ripper's true identity exist. And Sir William may have been institutionalized for quite different reasons.

Was Robert James Lees a psychic with true power? Did he lead police to the home of Jack the Ripper? Or was he a con artist attempting to gain publicity and more clients?

Those who are suspicious of Lees have at least three problems with his account. First, many of his statements cannot be verified. For example, criminologist Dr. Donald J. West asked Scotland Yard about Lees's story; they denied ever having spoken to Lees. Second, the police conducted a bizarre investigation. Long after Sir William had been confined to an institution, the police continued to question other suspects. If Sir William was Jack the Ripper, why did the police continue to search for him? Or did the police simply conduct a poorly coordinated investigation? Finally, many of the details contained in his account are incorrect. For example, Lees never stated whether he saw Sir William Gull or someone else the night that he was on the bus with his wife. Furthermore, the 12:40 A.M. time of one murder was inaccurate, since the early murders were committed after 2:00 A.M. And his account of "seeing" the last murder while eating dinner with his friends is also wrong, since the victim was killed late at night, not at the normal dinner hour Lees reported.

SKEPTICAT SAYS :

1. Lees's statements can't be proved. Scotland Yard denied them.

2. Why did police keep searching?

3. Lees never verified he saw Gull on the bus.

4. One murder did not happen at 12:40 a.m.

5. Lees couldn't have "seen" the murder while eating dinner unless he was eating after 2 a.m.!

..yeah. But...

Others, however, believe that these problems may be explained by the fact that he didn't write his account until forty years after the murders. The moral of this investigation is: a person involved in a psychic experience should record the events immediately, rather than wait years for memory to deteriorate and skepticism to multiply.

This was not the problem with a much more recent murder investigation, since this case was documented by an established (and inquisitive) children's author, Lois Duncan. Having written many young adult suspense novels (including *Summer of Fear*, *Killing Mr. Griffin*, and *Don't Look Behind You*), Duncan found herself involved in her own nightmarish case when her youngest daughter, eighteen-year-old Kaitlyn, was shot and killed one night while driving in her hometown of Albuquerque, New Mexico.

The police insisted that her death was simply the result of a random shooting, but Duncan and her husband, Don Arquette, began to doubt that analysis, especially after Kaitlyn's boyfriend, Dung, tried to commit suicide the day after her funeral. Duncan's oldest daughter, Robin, encouraged her to talk to a local psychic named Betty Muench who might be able to provide some clues about the death of Kaitlyn.

At first, Duncan resisted. Readers of her novels may be surprised that she was so hesitant, for she has written about telepathy, precognition, and other aspects of the paranormal. But she was not a strong believer in those subjects, only in the fact that they made her stories interesting and readable.

"I can't go to a psychic," she told Robin. "It just makes me sick to think about it." But Robin persisted, and eventually Duncan changed her mind.

Muench, who works free of charge on murder investigations, allowed Duncan to ask three questions:

1. What may I know about the well-being of Kaitlyn at this time and does she have a message for me?

2. What may I know about the circumstances of Kaitlyn's killing — about the car and any people involved?

3. What may I know at this time about the energy and identity of the killer, specifically the person, location, and present situation of this being?

The first question was suggested by Muench as a good way to begin a reading. The others, Duncan hoped, would provide more information about Kaitlyn's death. If these questions sound somewhat odd, remember that psychics work very differently from how they are portrayed on television and in movies. Most people in a similar circumstance would probably want to ask a direct question such as "Who killed my daughter?" and then expect the psychic to provide the killer's name and address. Notice that Duncan's questions are worded as polite requests (for example, "What may I know . . . ?"); they are the type of questions Betty Muench could answer best. As one psychic told Duncan at a later point during her investigation,

If I could come up with names and addresses . . . I'd be charging millions and living in style. Psychic detective work is based on impressions. The case is a jigsaw puzzle — you get a lot of pieces and you know they'll make a picture.

Betty Muench's answers, typed rapidly and nonstop on an electric typewriter, gave much more realistic (and therefore fuzzy) answers. Notice that the answers below (part of her responses to the second and third questions) would require considerable thought and investigation to piece together.

> There will be this that will show a kind of night image of two heads in the front of the vehicle and one short head in the back.
>
> There is this sense of an image which she gets so briefly that it is almost nonreal. This will seem to evoke some sort of recognition in her, and it is as if she is not afraid, someone she will seem to recognize and know. There will be no panic in her at this moment.
>
> There is a sense of three people involved and that . . . these will be split up and going in many directions now. There will be this energy which will show that one is going west and one is going south and the other is going northeast.

Muench went on to say that the car she saw was a "low rider," one often driven by teenagers.

Of course, an ESPrivate Eye might ask, was Muench using clairvoyance or telepathy to provide her answers? Although Duncan left the meeting believing in

Muench's clairvoyance, Muench may have been using telepathy to tap some information that Duncan already knew.

For example, before visiting Muench, Duncan learned that the police were looking for a gold "low rider" Camaro that a truck driver had seen chasing Kait's car shortly before she was killed. Telepathic communication between the two women would easily explain Muench's use of the term "low rider."

On the other hand, the police believed that only two people were in the Camaro. Muench saw three people, which implies her impression was clairvoyant — especially when the police later arrested three suspects in Kaitlyn's death, one of whom owned a gold Camaro.

Near the end of the reading Duncan gave Muench some personal items belonging to Kaitlyn. When she was handed Kaitlyn's watch, which she had worn on the night of her death, Muench said:

> I get a lot from watches. They absorb a great deal of energy, because people wear their watches all the time, not just on special occasions. Kait looked at this watch over and over that night. The time of nine o'clock was very strong in her mind. There's a sense of knowing where she was going, a destination she wanted to reach by nine. There's a suggestion of a kind of setup.

Duncan didn't understand why her daughter would have been concerned about the time, especially "nine o'clock." She had apparently spent the entire evening

167

with her friend Susan. She hadn't been shot until almost 11:00 P.M. But Muench had given her more puzzle pieces with which to work. And, although "nine o'clock" seemed meaningless, Duncan did discover that her daughter had had a secret meeting with someone and had not arrived at Susan's house until 9:30 P.M.

In all, Duncan had seven readings with Muench, and more with three other psychics. Every time the case seemed to run into a dead end, Duncan went for a reading to uncover additional clues. At one point, for example, the police had to drop charges against two of the three suspects. Frustrated, Duncan paid another visit to Muench. "There is a sense of Kaitlyn impressing with the letters R and J," she told Duncan.

Through her own inquiries and the work of a private detective, Duncan was able to determine that her daughter's boyfriend was working for a Los Angeles company named R & J Car Leasing that was involved in car insurance fraud. How could Muench have possibly known this? No one, not even the police, had known about the company or Dung's involvement with it.

What surprised Duncan most throughout the investigation was how she had apparently used precognition in selecting the details of her novels. For example, in *The Third Eye* she had created a character named Anne Summers who was a psychic. When Duncan met Betty Muench for the first time, she was stunned to see that Anne Summers's description fit Betty Muench perfectly. Had she looked into the future to see Muench?

During her investigation Duncan worked with a news-paper reporter who was instrumental in keeping the case alive and prodding the police to follow new leads. His name was Mike Gallagher. One night Duncan turned on the television and coincidentally saw the TV movie based on *Summer of Fear*. She had written the novel sixteen years earlier and didn't remember the plot or the characters well. As she watched, she was jolted by the name she had given to the heroine's boyfriend: Mike Gallagher. Could she have known that another Mike Gallagher would help her one day? Or was it just a coincidence involving a common name?

The last novel Duncan published before Kait's death, *Don't Look Behind You*, seemed to contain a number of surprising (and disturbing) precognitions. First, Duncan had modeled April, the main character, after Kaitlyn. Shortly before her death, Duncan had autographed Kait's copy: "For Kait, my own special 'April.' Always be sure to look behind you, honey!" Perhaps Duncan had had a sense that Kait would soon be in trouble.

Second, the police came to suspect a hit man named Miguel Garcia, nicknamed "Vamp," had been hired to kill Kait. In *Don't Look Behind You,* the name of the hit man hired to kill April is Mike Vamp. Finally, Lois Duncan created a scene in which Mike Vamp drives a gold Camaro to stalk April. The police were able to connect Miguel Garcia to a gold Camaro as well.

Although the psychic readings provided some useful puzzle pieces, they have not, so far, helped Duncan or the Albuquerque police solve the case. In fact, the charges against Miguel Garcia were dropped after he spent fifteen months in jail awaiting trial. However, Duncan now has a better understanding of the circumstances surrounding Kaitlyn's death, thanks to the details provided by many of the psychic readings *and* the way in which she connected them. A private investigator who worked for Duncan has proposed the following theory: When Kaitlyn discovered that her boyfriend and his friends were involved in a drug ring, she was killed.

But who killed her is exactly the question Duncan still wants answered; it explains why she wrote a book called *Who Killed My Daughter?* In it, she carefully detailed all of the information on the case, including the psychics' readings, in hopes that others with information to share would come forward. This is one of the most realistic glimpses of how psychics can help an investigation. Remember, though, that no speedy conclusion came about as a result of using psychics. The end of this puzzling story has not yet been written, but Lois Duncan has become so impressed with the psychics who assisted her and her own apparent precognitions that her next book may well be a nonfiction book about ESPower.

10. A Thoughtful Future

Have you ever set an alarm clock each night only to find yourself waking up a few minutes before the alarm rang morning after morning? Or have you ever needed to get up and didn't have an alarm clock? At bedtime, you might have said to yourself, "I want to get up at 7:00 A.M. tomorrow." Sure enough, at 7:00 A.M. you awoke.

If you've ever had these common experiences, you may not have realized how ESP may have already been working for you. Mr. W. van Vuurde of Cape Town, South Africa, was interested in his ability to awaken at precisely the right time each morning. He wondered if it was simply habit or if ESP was at work; he decided to perform a simple experiment.

173

Clock that stops when lever is pressed

Broken clock placed in box

For the experiment, he used two clocks. One was a regular alarm clock, which he altered so that by pressing a lever, he could stop the clock from working. The other clock had hands but was otherwise broken.

At bedtime, van Vuurde took the broken clock and, without looking at its face, spun the time-setting knob to a new time. Then, still without checking the face, he placed the clock in a box beside his bed.

"Wake me up at the exact time on the face of the broken clock," he told himself. Then he went to bed.

If he woke up during the night, he pushed the lever on the clock that worked, to record the time. Then,

when he woke at his regular time, he checked the times on the stopped clock and on the broken clock. He wrote

174

the two times down in a log book, making sure to keep a careful record of his experiment.

Van Vuurde had enough success that he sent his findings to Professor A. E. H. Bleksley of the University of the Witwatersrand in Johannesburg. Bleksley was so impressed that he wanted to continue the experiment under more refined circumstances — because of the simple nature of van Vuurde's experiment, the broken clock showed a time when van Vuurde would be awake (for example, nine o'clock) about one third of the nights.

Bleksley asked van Vuurde to send the broken alarm clock to him, nine hundred miles away. He would set the clock each night to a random time that fell within the usual eight hours that van Vuurde slept. Van Vuurde would continue to stop his clock at home each night when he awoke and record the time in a logbook the following morning. Bleksley decided that the experiment would continue for 284 nights, a number chosen at random. Then van Vuurde would send his log to the professor.

Bleksley was curious to learn what kind of success van Vuurde would have. By guessing alone, a person performing this experiment should succeed only once in five hundred tries. If that person had ESP, however, he or she would be able to wake up at the time on the broken clock's face many times.

How did van Vuurde do? Out of 284 nights, he stopped the clock correctly eleven times. That may not seem like many times, but the odds of this happening are 250,000 to one, and seem to rule out the possibility of luck. According to noted parapsychologist J. Gaither Pratt, "the results as a whole showed that [van Vuurde's] ESP told him occasionally what time had been set on the target clock."

Try your own version of
Van Vuurde's ESP
ALARM EXPERIMENT

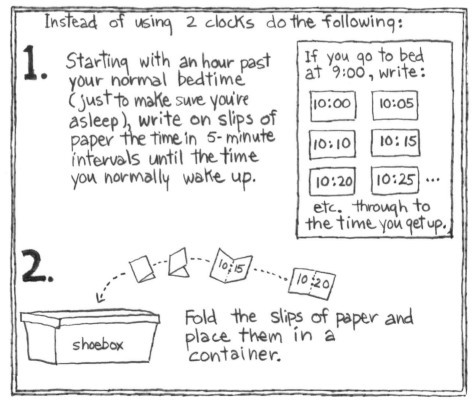

Instead of using 2 clocks do the following:

1. Starting with an hour past your normal bedtime (just to make sure you're asleep), write on slips of paper the time in 5-minute intervals until the time you normally wake up.

If you go to bed at 9:00, write:

| 10:00 | 10:05 |
| 10:10 | 10:15 |
| 10:20 | 10:25 | ...

etc. through to the time you get up.

2. Fold the slips of paper and place them in a container.

shoebox

3. Each night, select one slip of paper and, without <u>looking</u> <u>at it</u>, put it aside where no one will tamper with it.

4. Tell yourself you want to wake up at the time indicated on the paper.

Self, I want to wake up at the time on the slip.

5. Keep a notebook and pencil next to your alarm clock. If you wake up, jot down the exact time.

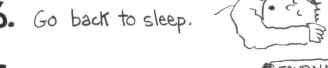

6. Go back to sleep.

7. Record the results in a journal.

JOURNAL

Conduct the experiment for at least a month. In 30 days' time, anyone could expect to wake up at the correct time at least once. The more times you wake up at the pre-selected time, the more you're providing evidence of your ESPower.

Of course, ESP can turn up in less normal circumstances. Take the case of Michael Wright, first reported by the psychiatrist Ian Stevenson.

One day, Dr. Stevenson received a phone call from Michael's mother, Catherine. She was concerned about some statements that her three-year-old son had made about someone named Walter Miller. Miller had once been a boyfriend of Mrs. Wright's. She had even been planning to marry him until he had been killed in a car accident. Now — some eleven years after his death — she was convinced that Walter Miller had been reincarnated as Michael.

The basic facts of this case may puzzle or even disturb you. You may also wonder how ESP could possibly be related to such an unusual story. Try to figure it out as you read the rest of the story.

Walter Miller and Catherine Wright had dated each other steadily throughout the first three years of high school. Walter was quite popular and known for his artistic ability. One night during the summer of 1967, Walter went to a dance without Catherine. There, he made the mistake of drinking, and on the way home, he fell asleep while driving. His car ran off the road, killing him instantly.

Catherine was stunned by his death but managed to get on with her life. Shortly after high school graduation, she married Frederick Wright. Around the time of her marriage, Catherine dreamed about Walter. In her

178

dream, according to Stevenson, "Walter said that he was not dead, as people thought, that he would come back, and that he would draw pictures for her again." Catherine, who believed in the idea of reincarnation, thought that Walter might be reborn — most likely as the child of his sister, Carole Miller Davis.

Catherine and Frederick Wright had two children: a daughter and then, in 1975, Michael. He seemed to be a normal child until the age of three. Then he exhibited characteristics associated with ESP.

"Carole Miller," he said to his mother quite unexpectedly one day. This was the maiden name of Walter's sister, a name that Michael had never heard. Carole had married long before Michael's birth and was only known to him by her married name, Carole Davis.

Another day Michael told his mother what happened to Walter Miller:

> A friend and I were in a car, and the car went off the side of the road and rolled over and over. The door came open, and I fell out and was killed.

Michael said that the windshield had shattered and that Walter's body had been carried over a nearby bridge. He also reported that Walter's friend, Henry Sullivan, had been in the car, too, though he was uninjured.

Dr. Stevenson agreed to interview Catherine Wright in person. During the interview, she showed him a newspaper article about the accident. The details that Michael reported were confirmed by the newspaper article: Walter had been thrown from the car. The impact, which broke his neck, killed him instantly. The ambulance that recovered his body traveled over a bridge near the accident. And Henry Sullivan had been a passenger in the car.

Reincarnation? Dr. Stevenson wasn't sure, although he found no reason to assume that Catherine Wright was lying. On the other hand, a case for telepathy rather than reincarnation can be made. Could Michael have read his mother's mind? Did he find the name "Carole Miller" in her thoughts? Did he "see" the accident as his mother thought about it?

From what is known about ESP, these ideas seem possible. On the other hand, Michael might have simply overheard his mother talk about these things (though she told Stevenson this had not happened) and remembered what she said.

Of course, neither possibility explains why Michael would talk as if he were Walter Miller. Could he have seen the dream of Walter Miller in his mother's mind?

Could he have overheard his mother tell someone about the dream?

Or could Michael have been the reincarnation of Walter?

Now that you've seen how puzzling and fascinating ESP really is, you may be ready to begin your own explorations. Will you dabble with the possibilities of telepathy, clairvoyance, and precognition? Will you try to read someone's mind or "see" what someone else is doing right now? Will you attempt to look into the future for a glimpse of what may be heading your way?

Or will you try to solve the mysteries of ESP by becoming a parapsychologist? Until you do, read as much as you can about the field of parapsychology and set up your own ESP experiments. Record your procedures and results with precision and care. Then reflect on your findings and decide what they show.

Such dedicated research can only help explain the enigma of ESP.

For Further Reading

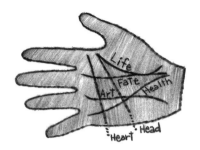

Arvey, Michael. *ESP: Opposing Viewpoints*. San Diego: Greenhaven, 1989.

Cohen, Daniel. *ESP*. New York: Messner, 1986.

———. *How to Test Your ESP*. New York: Dutton, 1982.

Hyde, Margaret O., Edward S. Marks, and James B. Wells. *Mysteries of the Mind*. New York: McGraw-Hill, 1972.

Kettlekamp, Larry. *Sixth Sense*. New York: Morrow, 1970.

Klein, Aaron E. *Beyond Time and Matter: A Sensory Look at ESP*. Garden City, N.Y.: Doubleday, 1973.

Acknowledgments and Bibliography

I wish to thank John LaMartine, librarian of the American Society for Psychical Research, for answering my many questions and suggesting valuable material.

The following is a list of the materials I found most useful in writing this book.

Angoff, Allan. *Eileen Garrett and the World Beyond.* New York: William Morrow, 1974.

Archer, Fred. *Crime and the Psychic World.* New York: William Morrow, 1969.

Ashby, Robert. *Guidebook for the Study of the Paranormal.* York Beach, Maine: Samuel Weiser, 1987.

Auerbach, Loyd. *Psychic Dreaming.* New York: Warner, 1991.

Blackmore, Susan J. *Beyond the Body.* London: Grafton, 1983.

Broughton, Richard S. *Parapsychology: The Controversial Science.* New York: Ballantine, 1991.

Davies, Rodney. *The ESP Workbook.* Wellingborough, England: Aquarian Press, 1987.

Dempsey, Tom Gene. *The Use of Psychics by Police as an Investigative Aid: An Examination of Current Trends and Potential Applications of Psi Phenomena to Law Enforcement.* Unpublished M.S. dissertation. California State University, Long Beach, 1981.

Dossey, Larry. *Meaning & Medicine.* New York: Bantam, 1991.

Duncan, Lois. *Who Killed My Daughter?* New York: Delacorte, 1992.

Eason, Cassandra. *The Psychic Power of Children.* London: Random Century, 1990.

Eysenck, Hans J., and Carl Sargent. *Know Your Own Psi-Q.* London: Corgi, 1986.

Feder, Kenneth L. *Frauds, Myths, and Mysteries.* Mountain View, California: Mayfield Publishing, 1990.

Garrett, Eileen J. *Many Voices.* New York: G.P. Putnam's Sons, 1968.

Gittelson, Bernard. *Intangible Evidence.* New York: Simon and Shuster, 1987.

Goodman, Jeffrey. *Psychic Archaeology.* New York: Berkley, 1977.

Gurney, Edmund; Myers, F. W. H., and Podmore, Frank. *Phantasms of the Living.* Edited by Mrs. Henry Sidgwick. New York: Dutton, 1918.

Halifax, Joan. *Shamanic Voices.* New York: Dutton, 1979.

Hansel, C. E. M. *The Search for Psychic Power.* Buffalo: Prometheus Books, 1989.

Haraldsson, Erlendur, and Joop M. Houtkooper. "Psychic Experiences in the Multinational Human Values Study: Who Reports Them?" *Journal of the American Society for Psychical Research,* April 1991, 145–165.

Heaps, Willard A. *Psychic Phenomena.* Nashville: Nelson, 1974.

Hearne, Keith. *Visions of the Future.* Wellingborough, England: Aquarian Press, 1989.

Hibbard, Whitney S., and Raymond W. Worring. *Psychic Criminology.* Springfield, Ill.: Thomas, 1982.

Huson, Paul. *How to Test and Develop Your ESP.* New York: Stein and Day, 1975.

Inglis, Brian. *The Paranormal: An Encyclopedia of Psychic Phenomena.* London: Grafton, 1986.

———. *The Unknown Guest.* London: Coronet, 1989.

Johnson, Martin. "Parapsychology and Education." In Betty Shapin and Lisette Coly (eds.), *Education in Parapsychology.* New York: Parapsychology Foundation, 1976.

Jones, David E. *Visions of Time*. Wheaton, Ill.: Theosophical Publishing House, 1979.

Krieger, Dolores. *Living the Therapeutic Touch*. New York: Dodd, Mead, 1987.

Krippner, Stanley, ed. *Extrasensory Perception*. Advances in Parapsychological Research, Volume 2. New York: Plenum Press, 1978.

Lyons, Arthur, and Marcello Truzzi. *The Blue Sense*. New York: Mysterious Press, 1991.

Mitchell, Edgar D. *Psychic Explorations*. New York: G. P. Putnam's Sons, 1974.

Myers, Frederic W. H. *Human Personality and its Survival of Bodily Death*. 2 vols. London: Longmans, Green, 1903.

Peterson, James W. *The Secret Life of Kids*. Wheaton, Ill.: Theosophical Publishing House, 1987.

Pratt, J. Gaither. *ESP Research Today*. Metuchen, New Jersey: Scarecrow Press, 1973.

———. *Parapsychology*. Metuchen, New Jersey: Scarecrow Press, 1977.

Prince, Walter Franklin. *Noted Witnesses for Psychic Occurrences*. New Hyde Park, N.Y.: University Books, 1963.

Psychics. New York: Harper & Row, 1972.

Rhine, J. B. *The Reach of the Mind*. New York: William Sloane, 1971.

Rhine, Louisa E. *ESP in Life and Lab*. New York: Collier, 1969.

———. *Hidden Channels of the Mind*. New York: William Sloane, 1961.

———. *The Invisible Picture*. Jefferson, North Carolina: McFarland & Company, 1981.

Rider, Carl. *Your Psychic Power*. London: Piatkus, 1988.

Rogo, D. Scott. *Psychic Breakthroughs Today*. Wellingborough, England: Aquarian Press, 1987.

Schlitz, Marilyn J., and Charles Honorton. "Ganzfeld Psi Performance Within an Artistically Gifted Population." *Journal of the American Society for Psychical Research*, April 1992, 83–98.

Schmeidler, Gertrude R. "Clairvoyance and Telepathy." In Ivor

Grattan-Guinness (ed.), *Psychical Research*. Wellingborough, England: Aquarian Press, 1982.

Schwartz, Stephan A. *The Alexandria Project*. New York: Delta, 1983.

———. *The Secret Vaults of Time*. New York: Grosset & Dunlop, 1978.

Stevenson, Ian. *Children Who Remember Previous Lives*. Charlottesville: University Press of Virginia, 1987.

———. "Precognition of Disasters." *Journal of the American Society for Psychical Research*, April 1970, 187–210.

———. *Telepathic Impressions*. Charlottesville: University Press of Virginia, 1970.

Tanous, Alex, and Timothy Gray. *Dreams, Symbols, and Psychic Power*. New York: Bantam, 1990.

Tart, Charles T. *PSI*. New York: Dutton, 1977.

Vaughan, Alan. *The Edge of Tomorrow*. New York: Coward, McCann & Geoghegan, 1982.

———. *Incredible Coincidence*. New York: Ballantine, 1989.

———. *Patterns of Prophecy*. New York: Hawthorn Books, 1973.

Williams, Stephen. *Fantastic Archaeology*. Philadelphia: University of Pennsylvania Press, 1991.

Wilson, Colin. *The Psychic Detectives*. San Francisco: Mercury House, 1985.

Index